Miss Stephen's
Apprenticeship

Robert D. Richardson, *series editor*

Miss Stephen's Apprenticeship

How Virginia Stephen Became Virginia Woolf

Rosalind Brackenbury

University of Iowa Press ❖ IOWA CITY

University of Iowa Press, Iowa City 52242
Copyright © 2018 by the University of Iowa Press
www.uipress.uiowa.edu
Printed in the United States of America

Design by Omega Clay

The University of Iowa Press is a member of Green Press Initiative and
is committed to preserving natural resources.

Printed on acid-free paper

Cataloging-in-Publication data is on file at the Library of Congress.
ISBN 978-1-60938-551-4 (pbk)
ISBN 978-1-60938-552-1 (ebk)

In memory of Ann L. McLaughlin

Contents

....

Acknowledgments

....

I would like to thank the writers and artists of Key West, Florida, who have become my friends and supporters over the last twenty years; particular thanks to Kathryn Kilgore for the Writers' and Artists' House, where for years some of us have been able to work in peace and privacy. We all need our communities.

Also, thanks posthumously to my friend, the French novelist and translator of Woolf's "Freshwater," Elisabeth Janvier, who left me her Virginia Woolf library.

Miss Stephen's
Apprenticeship

Introduction

In 1964, when I was twenty-two years old, I first opened Virginia Woolf's novel *The Waves*. I was on a bus, crossing the Downs at Epsom in the south of England, on my way to my first teaching job at a London school. In one of those flashes of understanding that occur rarely in life, I saw what fiction could do. "The sun had not yet risen. The sea was indistinguishable from the sky, except that the sea was slightly creased as if a cloth had wrinkles in it."

I looked out, in this book, on a landscape I had never seen before. In reality, I looked out from the upper windows of my bus across the gray-green curves of the Downs to the racetrack where the Epsom Derby is run, where at morning exercise small men perch high on the necks of their horses, the horses' breath visible in chill air. But the landscape of possible fiction also spread before me. Oh, so this is what you can do? This is how you can look at the world? This is how you can write?

· · · ·

The rest of my journey—the train to Clapham Junction, the dreary school with its asphalt grounds and children herded into bare rooms—didn't matter. I could write about it all in a way that would transform it. Virginia Woolf had given me permission. I took a notebook. I began again. *The Waves* was in my bag like a talisman—like a gift from one novelist to another, if I dared to take it.

It's an illusion, of course, that as a beginning writer you can launch yourself from the mature works of a writer of genius. But it's like seeing the world from space, or at least from an airplane. You get a sense of the whole picture and then spend a lifetime up close, trying to describe it. Perhaps it's an illusion we need, to be able to begin at all.

Finding a writer on your own is very different from being told what to read and how to read it. There's a private excitement about it: you have found a treasure, and it's yours alone. I had reached the age of twenty-two and had a university education without having read Virginia Woolf or even hearing of her; I know it sounds strange, but that is how it was. There are fashions in reading, and everyone I knew at college had been reading D. H. Lawrence (whom Woolf admired, though with reservations about his preachiness). Dr. F. R. Leavis was lecturing on him at Cambridge University in those years, and his canon had no room for Virginia Woolf. Eudora Welty had a similar experience of surprise and discovery when she picked up Woolf's *To the Lighthouse* in 1930 in Mississippi: "As it happened, I came to discover *To the Lighthouse* by myself. . . . Blessed with luck and innocence, I fell upon the novel that once and forever opened the door of imaginative fiction for me, and read it cold, in all its wonder and magnitude."

My parents thought it unnecessary to study your own language, and they believed that reading could be done in your spare time. I don't remember from what bookshelf I had taken this copy of *The Waves*, but it wasn't mine or theirs. Unlike Virginia Stephen's parents, mine did not focus entirely on their sons or think that a university education was unnecessary for a girl; but they did believe that it should lead somewhere useful. I hadn't been allowed to read English as a subject—although I did sneak in among friends to hear F. R. Leavis and George Steiner lecture. My actual degree was in history, followed by a postgraduate diploma in education at London. Now here I was on my way to my first (terrifying) teaching job. But I had *The Waves*. I had the Downs and the racehorses exercising and the whole way the sky lifted over the dull town of Epsom at eight-thirty in the morning; and hours later, as I made the same journey in reverse, I had the glint of sun on the windows of houses—which Woolf likened to fires. I had the way she made me see everything new.

Virginia Stephen taught herself to write. How did she do it? How did she become the great modernist that she was? What is it that convinces someone that she is a writer, and what allows her to become that writer? What provided her apprenticeship, and how did she come to think of herself as a writer and then a novelist?

Virginia made her own way; when her brothers were sent to Cambridge University to be educated, she and her sister Vanessa stayed at home. What series of connections and accidents led to those novels, the greatest of which she produced only in her middle age? What made Virginia Stephen into Virginia Woolf? With a writer who has been written about so much, these questions recur. The quest feels intimate—and hard.

Someone in a restaurant once asked me, "How did you know you were a writer?" It goes back to the deep gut feeling I had as a child while reading, the joyful yet alarming knowledge that this is me, this is what I can do. It may sound arrogant. But what if you feel you are meant to be a doctor, a musician, or a priest? You simply know. You know it as you know your own inner self; you don't know how to do it, of course, but you have your mission, as they say in the movie *Mission Impossible*, should you choose to accept it.

Reading was a vital part of Virginia Stephen's life. She grew up surrounded by books in the house at Hyde Park Gate. What she was reading provided a framework for her later life. She read in Greek, Latin, French and English, then began learning Italian. Leslie Stephen's daughter grew up with all the books around her that she needed. In 1903 she wrote to her brother Thoby, "I always read Montaigne in bed." And in the same letter she said of Euripides, "Bacchae is far and away the best." She read all the classics and the works of most of her contemporaries—some of whom received scathing mention in public ("my real delight in reviewing is to say nasty things") and in private ("reading Henry James is like being stuck like a fly in amber").

The movement from reading to writing may occur quickly or take years. Virginia Stephen knew what she wanted to do yet doubted her ability to do it. It's like watching a tennis player at Wimbledon or during the French Open: you can get up from the couch feeling sure that you too could become that good a player. But the way it is done is through learning, practice, never giving up, and trying different shots—hitting six balls over the net and hitting them back again, over and over, every day for the rest of your life. This is what Virginia did—not on a tennis court, of course, but on paper. Her mind tirelessly processed life, and her hand wrote it. There isn't an easy way to become this good at what you do, and she knew it from an early age. Everything she wrote is now in print, except for the contents of her wastebasket. You can trace her progress, reading about her self-doubts, her torments of self-consciousness, and her longing to be better than she was; you can follow the trains of thought, the days of illness, and the moments of excited inspiration that led in midlife to her greatest books.

But how did Virginia get there? Surely it wasn't just practice. Isn't there a hidden genius that some people have and others don't? In the chapters that follow I explore just what the balance may have been: slog and inspiration, influence and originality, hard work and the idea that comes floating in at the end of the day like a moth to a candle flame.

She began humbly, writing "descriptions" and book reviews. She also wrote hundreds of letters. I have gone back to her early letters, where I found a skittish, voluble Virginia, pouring out her life and ideas to her friend and confidante Violet Dickinson, along with her news of what she was reading, her doubts and fears about her own abilities, and the sheer love of gossip that would pervade her letters for the rest of her life.

From about 1902 she was writing steadily. Her first review was published in 1904. By this time, after her father's death, she was an orphan and was living with her three siblings at 46 Gordon Square; money was short, as it often was for her. But she had always had wider aspirations. Already in 1902 she wrote to Violet, "I'm going to write a great play which shall be all talk too. Im [sic] going to have a man and a woman—show them growing up—never meeting—not knowing each other—but all the time you'll feel them coming nearer and nearer. This will be the real exciting part—but when they almost meet—only a door between—you see how they just miss—and go off at a tangent and never come anywhere near again. There'll be oceans of talk and emotions without end."

In 1909 she wrote to Madge Vaughan, "Oh how I wish I could write a novel. People and their passions, or even their lives without passions, are the things to write about."

· · · ·

At a place and time like the United States today, in which the trajectory of a writer very often starts in the classroom of a master of fine arts program, it's instructive to ask, how did a great writer who had no formal education invent for herself the framework she needed for a writing life? How did she know what she had to learn? These days we are so used to the idea of learning from writing professors: teachers who may be, and often are, well-known writers themselves. We learn too from our contemporaries and colleagues, the other students in the program. If a writing student doesn't do the tasks set and doesn't show up for class, he or she will fail—that still happens, in spite of the notion held by some that everybody deserves a good grade.

I remember a student of mine whom I hunted down because she had simply disappeared and I was worried about her. She came raging to my room: "You set the dean on me! My life was impossible before that, now it's even worse!" She burst into tears, and as I handed her tissues she told me the story of what she had been dealing with. Write it, I said. Just damn well get it down. It was the most passionate piece of writing anyone brought to class that year, and she became the most committed student. If you teach writing, there are scenes like this, and students like this; who knows if they will go on to write this passionately for the rest of their lives? But Virginia Stephen only had her letters in which to pour out her frustrations; later she also had an unsympathetic, or at least nonunderstanding, doctor, who made her lie in bed, drink milk, and do no reading or writing for weeks on end. What a cure for a frustrated writer! I can hardly bear to imagine it.

The events of Virginia Stephen's childhood and adolescence were enough to provide her with both an intense anxiety about life and all the themes she would deal with in her novels. At six she had been fondled by one of her half brothers, George Duckworth, in the corridors of her father's house, and as a teenager she was approached more than once in her bedroom by her other half brother, Gerald Duckworth, who kissed and fondled her. Her mother, Julia, died when she was thirteen, followed by her much-loved half sister, Stella Duckworth (one of three children from Julia's first marriage); then her father, Leslie; then her older brother, Thoby. Death stalked many Victorian households, and it may be true that we are more easily shocked these days by sudden, early deaths simply because they are now rare. The orphaned Stephen children, living alone at Gordon Square, were at first a small, vulnerable society of four: Vanessa, Thoby, Virginia, and Adrian. After Thoby's death from typhoid at twenty-six, there were three. Then Vanessa married Clive Bell, and Virginia was left with her younger brother, the teenage Adrian.

All her life Virginia missed her mother. The loss of her obsessed and autocratic father was more ambiguous but equally devastating. The loss of Thoby echoes through her novels, most obviously *Jacob's Room*. The sudden death she metes out (mysteriously, in terms of the novel) to Rachel Vinrace in *The Voyage Out* echoes the death of Stella, her half sister: you fall in love, and you have to die. Mrs. Ramsay dies halfway through *To the Lighthouse*. Septimus Smith dies in *Mrs. Dalloway*. Percival (Thoby again) dies in *The Waves*.

The novels are tragedies, in effect. If life deals out the tragic, the seemingly inevitable deaths of people in an arbitrary fashion—isn't death always felt as arbitrary when you are young?—the novels are a writer's way of dealing with it. Virginia Woolf contained all the terror and beauty of life in her mature writing. Reading her, we reel from one to the other: the sheer beauty of the sun moving across the world in *The Waves*, the stunned little group of friends dealing with the death in youth of their beloved. How did Virginia do it? I think it was by simply not holding back. She paid a huge price, in terms of her own health, but that was partly the result of the inept medical practices of the time. She went down into the depths and dragged up what she found there: both treasure and bones.

But first she learned her trade, and it took her the best part of her youth and her maturity. That is what this book is about.

Expectations

It's a rare writer who has not been on the receiving end of at least some expectations, whether from family, friends, or at least one teacher. Often we need just one person to believe in us, to expect us to succeed. Virginia Stephen grew up in a highly literate family; her father, Sir Leslie Stephen, began editing the *National Dictionary of Biography* in the year she was born (1882), and his library was open to her from the moment she could read. He told visitors that "Ginia" would be a writer; but how this would happen, he did not specify. He wanted her to write to support his own work, and her first published piece of writing, in 1905, was in fact a memoir about him. It was written after his death, an anonymous contribution "by one of his daughters" to *Frederic Maitland's Life and Letters of Sir Leslie Stephen*. The work depressed her as much as it absorbed her, and it was dutiful and, inevitably, self-censored.

A letter to Thoby in 1896, when she was fourteen, has a postscript dictated by her father: "I want to see how quick this wretched girl can typewrite; I think she does it rather better than I had expected." In 1897 "this wretched girl" (possibly an affectionate appellation in disguise) wrote to Thoby, "The beauty of my language is sick, that I am driven to confess the reason o't—Mr. Payn sent father a book which is a great help to him (Mr. Payn) in his writings—called the Thesaurus of English Words—Perhaps you can explain Thesaurus—but the object of the work is to provide poor scant language authors with three or four different words for the same idea, so that their sentences may not jar—This father took as an insult, and accordingly handed it over to me—and I have been trying to make use of it."

In her next letter in the same year she told him, "My Dear Dr. Seton says I must not do *any* lessons this term." It was only two years after her mother's death, in 1895, and her own first mental breakdown. Struggling with the thesaurus, trying to impress her older brother, and "not doing any lessons," Virginia Stephen in her adolescence moved between very demanding expectations—studying Greek and Latin the same year at Kings College in London, attending history lectures there, and studying entomology at home with her father—and very low expectations.

In a letter to Vita Sackville-West in 1926, Virginia lampooned her upbringing. "Think how I was brought up! No school; mooning about alone among my father's books; never any chance to pick up what goes on in schools—throwing balls; ragging; slang; vulgarity; scenes; jealousies—only rages with my half-brothers, and being walked off my legs round the Serpentine by my father."

Janet Case, "regular as a Clock but a nice woman, really," as her student described her, was probably the most determined person in Virginia's surroundings to help her educate herself. Case, a Cambridge classicist, lived in Hampstead and gave Virginia lessons in Greek starting in 1902. She had a profound influence on Virginia, both intellectually and as a friend, and evidently put some structure into her life. When Leslie Stephen was dying in 1904, Virginia wrote to her, "Your talk is as good as a lesson." She was always slightly mocking of Case, as in this statement in a letter to Vanessa in 1908: "I had a letter from poor old Case. She is full of tender humanities and a kind of cultured Christianity, though she is too well educated to be a Christian." It was Case, a Cambridge graduate and scholar, who initiated Virginia into campaigning for women's suffrage and organized labor. She put the brakes on her student's excesses, it seems, and connected her with a wider, feminist worldview. In 1911 Virginia reported to Vanessa, "Janet C. said suddenly in the train, 'What are you thinking of, Virginia?' Imprudently I answered, 'Supposing next time we meet[,] a baby leaps within me?' She said that was not the way to talk."

When Leslie Stephen announced that his younger daughter would be a writer, he probably didn't mean a fiction writer, even though he was friends with novelists such as Thomas Hardy and Henry James, who both came to the house. The Victorian ideal of womanhood, as exemplified by his wife before her death, included much visiting of the poor, housekeeping, and attention to male well-being, especially his own. Virginia pinned this down forever in her description of Mr. Ramsay and his bids for his wife's attention in *To the Lighthouse*, written well after her father's death. Mr. Ramsey has just told his wife, rather brutally, that she won't finish the stocking she is knitting that night in time for him to take it to the lighthouse keeper's little boy the next day. "He wanted something—wanted the thing she always found it so difficult to give him; wanted her to tell him that she loved him. And that, no, she could not do."

What Virginia's demanding, emotionally dependent father wanted, at Hyde Park Gate in those days, was usually what came about. Virginia wrote to her friend Emma Vaughan in 1900, with some apprehension, "Thoby is here today but he goes tomorrow and then I shall be left alone with my Parent." In a letter the same year to George Duckworth she wrote, "Father is stretched at full length snoring on the sofa and this annoys me so much I can't write sense." Her father was not an easy companion, especially in his bereavement.

Parental expectations aside—and Leslie Stephen's for his younger daughter were a mixed bag—Virginia was expected to be literate, even learned, by the standards of her time. By the time she was eighteen she was reading in four languages. She was (vaguely) expected to marry and, in due course, have children. Vanessa, who married soon after their father's death and quickly got pregnant, was always an example and an inspiration to her, but one she felt unable to live up to. Her expectations of herself as an artist as well as a woman were colored by Vanessa's example, and she always felt inferior, or at least somehow unfinished by comparison. Being childless compounded this feeling. In 1907, when her sister was pregnant for the first time, she wrote to Violet Dickinson, "Nessa is like a great child, more happy and serene than ever, sketching . . . draped in a long robe of crimson, or raspberry, coloured silk." She added wistfully, "Shall I ever bear a child, I wonder?"

Thoby, at Cambridge, wrote to his younger sister as an intellectual equal and added suggestions to her reading list. His expectations of her were evidently high. In 1901 she wrote to him, "Father has begun to say 'We must talk about what you are to read at Fritham.' I have told him that you have promised to help me with a Greek play or two—Sophocles I think. . . . I have read the Antigone, Oedipus Coloneus—and am in the middle of the Trachiniae. I should rather like to read the Antigone again—and any others you advise. I find to my immense pride that I really *enjoy* not only admire Sophocles." Thus Thoby, whose education at public school and the university was considered worth paying for, passed on some of it—saving his father money, incidentally—to his younger sister.

It was usual then for girls to be educated at home. My own grandmother and two of my great-aunts, daughters of the master of an Oxford college, were allowed to go to Girton College at Cambridge at the same time that Virginia Stephen's education was being overseen by her father. But this was unusual, and they were still not allowed to earn degrees, as the men did, nor did they live on campus; instead they were segregated three miles out of town and brought to lectures in a covered horse-drawn carriage. My grandmother once asked permission to invite her father to tea in her rooms with a friend of hers and was told that she must have a chaperone. "But he's my father!" she protested, and got the reply, "But he's not the other girl's father." Some of the same prudishness and caution ruled in the Stephen household—but it was blown out the window by the Stephen children when they were orphaned by their father's death and left free to do as they liked in their house in Gordon Square.

Virginia was expected to be educated, dutiful, marriageable, and childbearing, as were all young women of her class and time. But her father's focus on her intellectual development and her devotion to him, to the point of neglecting all other aspects of her life, is more interesting. She had been given her marching orders, and march she did.

Unlike most contemporary young writers, she never thought of rushing straight into writing a novel. She knew what she had to learn first. Even though the idea of a play with "oceans of talk and emotions without end" excited her, as noted in the introduction, when she wrote to Violet Dickinson about it in 1902 she knew that she had to work toward it. She taught herself, writing reviews, pieces she called descriptions, and, above all, letters. She also taught herself by reading. During the years up to 1912, when she met and married Leonard Woolf and sent her first novel to Duckworth Press (owned by her half brothers) for publication, she was digging information from every book she read as well as honing her own descriptions of nature, people, conversations, and states of mind, working through flights of imagination and fantasy to find the exact word, excise the excesses, and arrive where she needed to be.

She questioned herself, challenged herself, and allowed others to challenge her. The letters she wrote to Clive Bell after his marriage to her sister show how she was calming herself down, organizing her mind so that she could write, preparing herself for the long haul of the novel. Her own expectations changed, as she moved from her despairing exclamation in 1909, "Oh how I wish I could write" (see introduction), to the assured "He has written a novel and so have I" after her marriage to Leonard in 1912. But was her novel any good? Would Leonard's be more favorably received? What would Morgan (E. M.) Forster, Tom (T. S.) Eliot, and her sister, Vanessa, think of it? Her own doubts and fears never quite left her. The legacy of Leslie Stephen, his fierceness and his expectations, remained with her long after his death; only decades later, with the publication of *To the Lighthouse*, did she finally lay him out in fiction and cast him metaphorically afloat.

What we expect of ourselves very often has its origins in the expectations of others: the voice in the ear, parental or otherwise, telling us what we should be doing or that we are not doing enough. Virginia Stephen grew up doing battle with her father's ghostly voice, and she admitted later that if he had lived to be ninety-six (rather than seventy-one), she would not have written her novels.

"I dont [sic] think I will come for dinner," she wrote to Violet Dickinson in 1902, "but to tea, as all 4 males are at home and I cant [sic] very well be out for dinner." Not only was she needed to preside over dinners and tea tables after her mother's death; there was also the unspoken command of what was suitable for a woman to write. Biography and essays were all right. In 1902 she wrote to Thoby, "My mind is dazed with Sidney Lee. He has come to consult about the Dictionary (How I wish it at the bottom of the sea!) and his squeak sounds like a tormented Rat." If Leslie Stephen had lived longer, would his daughter have been made to be just one more of the *Dictionary of National Biography's* acolytes?

Meanwhile, after his wife's death, Sir Leslie roamed the house groaning aloud, chanting poetry, as Mr. Ramsay does in *To the Lighthouse*, and when he too became sick, he needed both his daughters' permanent presence as well as a nurse. On the day after his death in February 1904, Virginia wrote to Janet Case, "All these years we have hardly been apart, and I want him every moment of the day." His influence was powerful, as that of strong-minded fathers tends to be for their daughters: the model and the oppressor, one to respect and the other to resist. The push and pull of tyranny is felt by Cam in the last pages of *To the Lighthouse*. It was not surprising that Virginia Stephen's expectations of herself were so high that she thought she never lived up to them, and that even at the height of her fame and success she could never let herself off the hook of self-criticism.

Thus the ideal of apprenticeship—to learn from a master or mistress of one's art, to work alongside a practicing artist—was for Virginia Stephen not straightforward. She had many mentors, and much was expected of her, but in a rather vague way. Women's careers were not, at the beginning of the twentieth century, considered important. So it was hard for women themselves to take a career seriously and to carve out the time and space in which to pursue it. Nevertheless, Vanessa was allowed to study painting with the notoriously ferocious Henry Tonks at the Slade School of Fine Art. Among her fellow students were young men who became ardent advocates of postimpressionism. She went to lectures by Roger Fry, who was on the opposite side from Tonks in the postimpressionist debate.

Vanessa therefore at least had a structure within which to learn. For Virginia, apprenticeship was largely to herself and to the writers of the past. The writer had to find her own way, whereas the painter had some formal instruction and, perhaps even more important, fellow students. This remained true for writers throughout most of the century, at least in England. The American master of fine arts is now duplicated in many British universities, but the first British "writing school" was started only in the 1960s under the aegis of Malcolm Bradbury and Angela Carter at the University of East Anglia in Norwich. Most British writers of the postwar generation were still in a position similar to Virginia Stephen's, finding inspiration, mentorship, and time to write where they could.

Reading

In a house full of books, reading was, of course, the one approved occupation for the Stephen children. Vanessa remembered Virginia reading aloud to her as she painted and drew; they read most of the Victorian novelists together in this way, and she could still hear much of George Eliot and William Thackeray in her sister's voice.

Julia Stephen had read aloud to her children—just as Mrs. Ramsey, throughout the first section of *To the Lighthouse*, reads aloud a story about a fisherman to her six-year-old son, James. But Julia preferred to make up her own stories, usually little morality tales of a rather banal cheerfulness. She liked to knit and tell a story as she did so. It was to Sir Leslie's library that Virginia went at a young age to find books.

I think that writers read in a different way from most people. There is really no such thing for a writer as reading for escape or entertainment; writers read to find out what other writers have done and then to discover what they themselves might do. Reading for them is a perpetual investigation; its eternal question is, if so-and-so has done this, then what can I do? Writers learn from other writers. They learn how to be themselves by closely observing others. It's like the way a child learns to talk—or, indeed, do anything.

In her youth Virginia Stephen read ambitiously and under orders. In her teens, she read Thomas Carlyle, "my beloved Macaulay," Charles Lamb's *Essays of Elia*, Samuel Pepys, and Michel de Montaigne. She loved the Elizabethan adventurer

Richard Hakluyt's tales and John Gibson Lockhart's *Life of Scott*. In one year, 1897, she read George Eliot's *Adam Bede* and *Felix Holt*, Charlotte Brontë's *Shirley*, Anthony Trollope's *Barchester Towers*, Elizabeth Gaskell's *North and South* and *Wives and Daughters*, and Nathaniel Hawthorne's *The Scarlet Letter*. Many of these were read aloud to Vanessa. Beginning in 1897, her main study was of the classics—first at the Ladies' Department of King's College, in Kensington, then in private lessons with classicist Clara Pater, and in 1898 with Janet Case, her mentor in Hampstead.

Thoby was a strong influence when he was an undergraduate at Cambridge, urging her to read William Shakespeare, whom she had compared unfavorably with the Greeks. She obeyed him, and after reading *Cymbeline* wrote to him in 1901, "Imogen says—'Think that you are upon a rock, and now throw me again'—and Posthumous answers—'Hang there like fruit, my soul, till the tree die.' Now, if that doesn't send a shiver down your spine, even if you are in the middle of cold grouse and coffee!" "Hang there like fruit, my soul!" was a favorite phrase of hers, quoted more than once in letters to her friends.

In 1906, reading the poetry of John Keats, she wrote to Violet Dickinson, "I think he is about the greatest of all—and no d——d humanity. I like cool Greek Gods and amber skies and shadow like running water, and all his great palpable words—symbols for immaterial things." The same year she wrote to Clive Bell, "I have been reading a book which I should tell you to read but that I don't want a snub—'My dear good Virginia, when I was a boy of 20' . . . and so on. At any rate, it is the Life of Sidney by Greville. And if there are such books in the world, I shall continue to live and read."

Her enthusiasm for what she was reading did not abate, even if she delivered scant praise at times; "cheerful manly books, Stevenson and Thoreau" were found on the bookshelves of a country cottage she and Adrian rented near Rye in 1907. Her program for her reading remained serious and thorough—even if she admitted to Clive Bell in 1908, when she was reading G. E. Moore's *Principia Ethica*, "I am climbing Moore like some industrious insect, who is determined to build a nest on the top of a Cathedral spire."

Looked at from the point of view of the twenty-first century, this was quite a program. Are any of us this well-read today? I doubt it. There was a thoroughness to the Victorian ideal of education—whether it was the study of flowers, birds, insects, music, or literature—that we simply don't have in this century. My grandmother and her sisters could name every plant they found on their afternoon walks, and they recognized every English bird by its song. Today there are far fewer plants and birds to name, and we have forgotten, or never even learned, the names of the survivors.

Reading was thorough in the same way. It was a way to form one's mind and opinions, to discriminate, weigh arguments, and judge truth. It was a serious occupation. What have we put in its place? The Internet? Digital mastery they would not have dreamed of? Yet writers still write. Readers, though fewer of us, perhaps, still read. We don't read as thoroughly or as exhaustively, and we don't like to tax our minds. Our writing has probably suffered. Our homes don't usually house extensive libraries—but we have our screens, and free downloads of the classics, if we choose. It's a very different era, more than a century since Virginia Stephen was growing up in her father's house at 22 Hyde Park Gate, and, of course, she had a privileged childhood.

What can we learn from Virginia's lifelong practice of such thorough and thoughtful reading? It was what made her the writer she became, at least in part. She trained her mind to think. She had tutors and educated brothers and friends, but essentially she took on this training herself. There were numerous writers who came before her, like the French writer George Sand, who wrote volumes about her ancestors before she wrote about herself. Virginia was conscious of them as precursors, as minds making up a tradition and a civilization within which she herself would eventually write.

Yet there was also an element of loneliness in her reading when she was young. When there is nobody to talk to, books fill the gap. In 1903 she wrote to Thoby at Cambridge, "I dont [sic] get anyone to argue with me now, and feel the want. I have to delve from books, painfully and all alone, what you get every evening sitting over your fire and smoking your pipe with [Lytton] Strachey etc. No wonder my knowledge is scant. There's nothing like talk as an educator, I'm sure." Wasn't this the whole difference between the education allowed to young men—and a few privileged women—and that granted to the "daughters at home," even of highly educated men, at the turn of that century? It's the whole argument in favor of university education: that it should be a place for the vivid and personal exchange of ideas. Even if "Strachey etc." and Thoby, smoking by the fire, did not always talk at the high level imagined by Virginia, they had the opportunity to do so. They were enjoying the leisure and companionship thought suitable for gentlemen—and gentlemen's talk, as everyone knew, was vastly superior to that of ladies. This longing to be at the fireside with her brother and his friends was what fired Virginia Woolf to write much of her feminist nonfiction, especially *A Room of One's Own* and *Three Guineas*. Intellectual loneliness struck her hard when Thoby died suddenly in 1906 at the age of only twenty-six. He was her mentor, her contemporary, and her leader in the field.

When Virginia met Leonard Woolf and married him in 1912, they embarked on a lifetime not just of structured and passionate reading but also of talk. At their house in Rodmell in Sussex, I saw their rather uncomfortable-looking chairs placed where they used to sit, one on each side of the fire. After a day of reading and writing, there was always the need, and the time, for talk. It was what they did together, and it cemented their marriage.

Virginia wrote to Thoby at Cambridge in 1903, "You are an angel to have routed out a Montaigne for me. I was getting quite desperate. I have hunted him 3 years." Michel de Montaigne, the French nobleman and essayist, was her lifelong companion. He was an incurable optimist—a man who left the door of his castle unlocked while unpaid starving mercenary soldiers were rampaging through the French countryside. His early influence on the young Virginia may well have been the voice of reason and cheerfulness that counterbalanced her father's temperament. Montaigne wasn't positive about women being sufficiently evolved to be able to sustain friendship, but perhaps she overlooked that part. Terrible things happened around him—he lost a dear friend to sudden illness and his country was in ruins—and he himself suffered the considerable pain of gallstones. Yet his voice remains, across the intervening centuries, mostly modest, humorous, and ironic.

Why would Virginia read Montaigne before going to sleep, alone in her room, while her father groaned and paced in the rather grim house at Hyde Park Gate in the 1890s, if not to get a regular dose of that calm sanity? If you try reading him in bed as Virginia did, you will end (or start) your day with a voice of moderation in your head. Nothing is intrinsically bad or good to him, but thinking, as Shakespeare also said, makes it so. "Even in virtue, our ultimate aim—no matter what they say—is pleasure," Montaigne wrote, as well as "I want death to find me planting my cabbages." His voice strikes us as modern in its relativism and its acceptance of foibles, starting with his own. The form of his essays, mostly very brief, suits the moments before falling sleep (or after waking up).

Readers know that what we read affects how we experience the world. We can create a climate in our brains this way —just as watching the TV news or a horror movie may give us a sleepless night. We read not just for information but for company—to join a vast existing company of other minds, most of them more experienced than our own. Many readers don't feel the urge to write. But those of us who are writers need other minds to grow with, just as we would never learn to speak without others who speak to us. We need to grow within a language, within a framework, on the map of human experience expressed in words. We need other minds in a very specific way—not just to explain the world to us, calm us down, or inform us but also to show us where we belong on the map, to enable us to find our own path.

Yet reading for Virginia Woolf was never confined to the classics, or books deemed to be "good." She was all in favor of omnivorous reading, perhaps on account of having been allowed to gobble up books freely in her father's library. We also need, she wrote, "trivial ephemeral books. They are the dressing-rooms, the workshops, the wings, the sculleries, the boiling cauldrons where life seethes and steams and is forever on the boil." We can't always be reading great books. "I ransack public libraries and find them full of sunk treasure." Of her old friend and mentor Janet Case, she wrote in her diary, "All her generation use their brains too scrupulously upon books, seeking meaning rather than letting themselves run on for pleasure, which is more or less my way."

The argument is for a culture of books, an ambience in which random reading can bring surprising and serendipitous treats—browsing, trying things out. Virginia was a lifelong supporter of public libraries and the democratic pleasures of their stacks. Only by reading widely can readers situate themselves in the wider culture. When Virginia Stephen was young, the wider culture was far more inclusive of history and language than that experienced by most young people today. She read French, Latin, and Greek authors as well as obscure women's memoirs, romances, stories of adventure and exploration, and whatever else she found in the libraries and bookshops at hand.

The voracious reading of her younger days gave way to more organized reading, mostly under the pressure of writing book reviews and then of reading manuscripts for the Hogarth Press. There was always a pile of books waiting: "Oh dear, what a lot I've got to read! The entire works of Mr James Joyce, Wyndham Lewis, Ezra Pound, so as to compare them with the entire works of Dickens & Mrs Gaskell; beside that George Eliot; & finally Hardy." Whether she actually read "the entire works" is not recorded.

One learns to read fast and absorb a book's essence through having to write regular reviews. The precocious Virginia, summoned to give an account of her reading by a demanding parent, was proud of her ability to read and judge. She cultivated this skill throughout her life, while—perhaps because of—living in dread of what reviewers might say of her own work. Of all the glowing reviews of her novel *Night and Day* that she received, it was Forster's that she seized on: "I like it less than *The Voyage Out* . . . none of the characters in *Night and Day* is lovable." She recorded that he told her this in person. But then they went for a walk along the riverbank together, and "suddenly out comes the obvious thing that one has overlooked. He is in trouble with a novel of his own, fingering the keys but only producing discords so far."

Reviewers can't help bringing their own writing to a review; nobody is objective. How we read each other and what we write about each other are subject to all the currents of envy, frustration, and confusion that a writer undergoes. We read, we write, we judge; all the while we are secretly judging ourselves. We try for objectivity—and fail.

3

Writing

This chapter examines three kinds of writing by Virginia Woolf: letters, diaries, and essays and reviews.

LETTERS

The first surviving piece of writing by Virginia Stephen is a letter written in 1888, when she was only six years old, to James Russell Lowell, prompted by her father: "My dear godpapa, have you been to the adirondacks and have you seen lots of wild beasts and a lot of birds in their nests you are a naughty man not to come here good bye yours affect. virginia."

During her teenage years, her letters were wild, witty, ridiculous, full of flourishes and private jokes, and sometimes decorated with cartoon drawings by Vanessa of "Miss Jan," as Virginia called herself. She wrote to Thoby, whom she called "Your Mightiness and Milord" or "My dear Grim," all the time he was away at Trinity College at Cambridge. On the receipt of some camera film, she wrote to him in 1897, "A thousand thanks (as the French say) [to] my dear Herbert for this munificent gift—I shall devote not a few to your remarkable face." She wrote screeds to her friend Violet Dickinson from 1902 on, and the writing grew whimsical, girlish, and exaggerated as they adopted the nicknames of animals. She also did this with Emma Vaughan, whom she addressed as "dearest Toad." Virginia signed herself "Sparroy," "yr. loving Goat," "Goatus," and "Il Giotto." She addressed Violet as "My woman," "My child," "My Aunt," or simply "Woman."

Her correspondence with Violet went from mawkish to monosyllabic, flirtatious to condemnatory; it's as though she were trying out all the moods and styles of her mercurial nature on this obliging older woman. "Sparroy says it's a question of DV [Deo Volente, "God willing"] whether shes [sic] in for tea tomorrow," she wrote in 1906. "Misery sits on her doorstep. Uncle dying—in fact dead . . . dressmaker incompetent—Sparroy not what you would call a strict woman of business. But Hell Cat rakes up the embers of my burnt heart—why are you flirting with old [Aunt] Minna [Duckworth]?" Letters like this are probably not what anyone would choose to have kept for posterity, let alone quoted. Virginia, impulsive as ever, was simply pouring out on paper whatever came to her. But they show her increasing fluidity and flexibility with language, her ability to flit from one mood to another, to shift topics and marry unlikely themes. They have a vibrant, if catty, virtuosity and are different in tone from the letters she wrote to Thoby and later to Clive Bell, her brother-in-law; they are all about exploring the limits and latitudes of female friendship with someone mature enough not to take offense.

Most remarkable, and hard to read without flinching, are the letters she wrote to Violet after Thoby's death. Violet herself was ill, and Virginia justified her lies by claiming she was sparing her friend anxiety. Thoby died on November 20, 1906, yet she wrote to Violet, on December 10, "Thoby is going on well, he has chicken broth of a kind, and will be up by Christmas" and, on December 12, "He begins to curse a good deal and points out the virtues of a mutton chop." It's an astonishing deception. Wishful thinking, anguish put at bay—whatever it was, she allowed Violet to believe for nearly a month after Thoby's death that he was getting better every day. Virginia fed her convincing details, all invented: his temperature, his meals, his remarks to the doctor. Moreover, she allowed herself to write about Thoby as if he really were alive, as though she believed it herself. It must have been a consoling exercise for an inconsolable sister.

On December 18 she asked Violet, "Do you hate me for telling so many lies? You know we had to do it. You must think that Nessa is *radiantly happy* and Thoby was splendid to the end." Fiction could mend; fiction could improve on life. Fiction could almost make you believe that death did not exist. In fact, Violet learned about Thoby's death only through reading a review in the *National Review of Books* of Frederic Maitland's *The Life and Letters of Leslie Stephen*.

The "radiantly happy" idea covered Virginia's initial feeling that Clive Bell was not worthy of her sister. Yet after Vanessa's marriage to Clive in 1907, a correspondence began between Virginia and her brother-in-law that contained some of the intellectual companionship she had shared with Thoby, with a good measure of open flirting, under the pen names of James Hatherly and Eleanor Hadying. Between treating him to sentences about slipping off one's silk dress and curling up in a dressing gown for the prosecution of an intimate, emotional, and, as she privately admitted, often irrational friendship, she trusted him with her questions and doubts about her manuscript "Melymbrosia" (which became her first novel, *The Voyage Out*). In 1909 she wrote the following to him:

> When I read the thing over (one very grey evening) I thought it so flat and monotonous that I did not even feel "the atmosphere"; certainly there was no character in it. Next morning I proceeded to slash and rewrite, in the hope of animating it; and (as I suspect—I have not reread it)—destroyed the one virtue it had—a kind of continuity; for I wrote it originally in a dreamlike state, which was, at any rate, unbroken. My intention now is to write straight on, and finish the book; and then, if that day ever comes, to catch if possible the first imagination and go over

the beginning again with broad touches, keeping much of the original draft and trying to deepen the atmosphere—Giving the feel of running water, and not much else. I want to bring out a stir of live men and women, against a background. I think I am quite right to attempt it, but it is immensely difficult to do. Ah, how you encourage me! It makes all the difference.

We don't know how Clive responded, but he was not a novelist, so perhaps he was a safer confidant than Lytton Strachey, to whom she wrote brief letters with invitations to tea and who evidently preferred the topic of his own work, even though he did propose marriage to her in a moment of confusion.

To Lady Robert Cecil ("my dear Nelly"), a writer of reviews to whom Virginia sent some of her own manuscripts for comment, she wrote some of the most interesting letters of her youth, moving away from her early frivolity to a calmer, though still ironic and playful tone. In 1909 she outlined an idea that was oddly prescient for the distant future in which we live: "There should be threads floating in the air, which would merely have to be taken hold of, in order to talk. You would walk about the world like a spider in the middle of a web. In 100 years [sic] time, I daresay these psychical people will have made all this apparent—now seen only with the eye of genius." She then complained, "Now Swinburne is dead, Meredith dumb, and Henry James inarticulate, things are in a bad way. . . . Nelly wont [sic] publish her novel and Virginia Stephen knows nothing about humanity." As she often did, Virginia launched her little barbs of self-criticism, hoping that her correspondent would contradict her. She wanted affection, and admiration, always. "I hope you are well, and fond of me."

Virginia wrote to Violet Dickinson in 1905, "Writing is a divine art, and the more I write and read the more I love it." She also asked Violet rather wistfully, "Do you think I shall ever write a really good book?" To Madge Vaughan in 1906 she wrote, "It seems to me to be better to write about the things I do feel, than to dabble in things I don't understand in the least. . . . That is the kind of blunder—in literature—which seems to me ghastly and unpardonable: people, I mean, who wallow in emotions without understanding them." In her letters to her friends, particularly close female friends, she risked being contradictory and illogical, feeling her way and allowing herself to try out ideas and attitudes. What was it that she was aiming for? She knew and did not know, glimpsed it and let it go again. I think again of the "great play" she had outlined to Violet in 1902, "which shall be all talk" (see introduction). The idea of the man and the woman who nearly meet but don't ("only a door between") is such a portent of her later novels, such a taste of the method she was later to find ("oceans of talk and emotions without end"). She never wrote that play, but the idea seems to infuse so much of her more mature work. Perhaps writers, even when young—she was twenty at the time—always have a feeler out in front of them, for what may come.

DIARIES

As well as writing the hundreds of letters that have survived, Virginia Stephen wrote "descriptions," then reviews of books, and then essays on various topics. In 1904 she confessed to her friend Lady Robert Cecil (Nelly): "When I see a pen and ink I cant [sic] help taking to it, as some people do to gin." She was also writing her diary, as so many Victorians did, but this did not become a conscientious daily habit until 1915, according to Leonard Woolf in his edition of her diaries.

In January 1897, just as she was about to turn fifteen, an age at which one can feel that life is just beginning, she started a journal of the new year. "The first really *lived* year of my life." She wrote it without a break, except for the day after her half sister Stella's death in July, after which it began to dwindle until she wrote, "Never mind, we will follow this year to its end & then fling diaries & diarising into a corner—to dust & moths & all creeping crawling eating destroying creatures." It must have seemed as if that first "really lived year," recorded, could in the end only record heartbreak or go silent. She restarted the diary habit several times between 1898 and 1915, writing in notebooks at first and jotting down observations about events and people but not about her own state of mind; only in 1905 did she begin a more formal diary again, deciding to write down her day-to-day musings and reflections. But this diary too was interrupted six weeks after its beginning by a worse mental breakdown than any she had suffered so far, a year after her father's death. Once again, how do you record heartbreaking loss—but how can you leave it out? The diary, begun again in 1915 and continuing almost without a break for the rest of her life, has very little in it about her own feelings, except about her writing. It's resolutely set in day-to-day life, and its attention is on the world rather than on herself. In a conversation with the aristocrat and literary hostess Ottoline Morrell about diaries, she mocked Ottoline for talking about her "inner" life and the diarizing of it; Virginia commented that she herself didn't think she had an inner life.

Her diaries are now available, published in their entirety, but a shortened diary, expurgated of all that was not directly related to her writing, came out under Leonard Woolf's editorship in 1954. "The diary is too personal to be published as a whole during the lifetime of many people referred to in it" was Leonard's judgment. He continued, "She was, I think, a serious artist—and all her books are serious works of art. The diaries at least show the extraordinary energy, persistence and concentration with which she devoted herself to the art of writing and the undeviating conscientiousness with which she wrote and rewrote and again rewrote her books."

What Virginia called life writing was to occupy her for her lifetime, and it was begun in her early journals in addition to her letters. The life writer explored the space between the outer self (which she considered a mask) and the inner, noticing self (which she sometimes called the soul). Even when young, Virginia Stephen knew about this gap: it was the distance between the Virginia who served tea to her father and his guests and the girl who wrote in her room late at night. This gap, or space, contained freedom: to change gender, to time-travel, to be outrageous, and to imagine widely. It was the space that eventually gave birth to *Orlando*.

ESSAYS AND REVIEWS

Virginia's first published essay came out in the *Guardian* in 1904 (not the *Manchester Guardian*, which became the liberal-minded British newspaper we know today, but a rather High Church clerical journal). The journal had already published her review of a novel by the American William Dean Howells. The essay, entitled "Hayworth," was about the Brontës at Hawick; she had been staying with her old friend Madge Vaughan on the Yorkshire moors, not far from the Brontës' house, when she wrote it. The journal took three more articles from her that year. She was delighted to be able to "keep myself in pocket money," as she wrote to Violet Dickinson in 1905. In the early months of that year she began to contribute to the *Times Literary Supplement*, the *National Review*, and the *Academy*.

In 1904, when one of her articles had been refused by the *Guardian*, she wrote to Violet, "I don't want Mrs. L's [Kathleen Lyttelton, the editor] candid criticism. I want her cheque! I know all about my merits and failings better than she can from the sight of one article, but it would be a great relief to know that I can make a few pence easily in this way—as our passbooks came last night and they are greatly overdrawn. . . .

But there is a knack of writing for newspapers which has to be learnt, and it is quite independent of literary merits." She also admitted to a very unprofessional approach to the first article—rejected—that she sent to Lyttelton, who was a friend of Violet's and so probably less critical than she might have been of Virginia's slapdash first effort. "I stupidly didn't type-write it—indeed, wrote it myself rather hurriedly and illegibly as I hate copying—and forgot to give my address, or to enclose a stamped envelope for return. So I dont [sic] think my chances are good."

Virginia went on to learn the "knack," for she felt somewhat responsible for the Stephen family's overdrawn bank account after the expenditures on doctors and nurses during her illness. "I must toil at the [Leslie Stephen] letters," she told Violet in 1904. "Then I have to write something for him [Frederic Maitland] before he sails . . . however that can wait—and a cheque or two wouldn't come amiss." So the need to make money at writing was instilled early, and Virginia was proud all her life when "a cheque or two" came in, even when she and Leonard were making good money with the Hogarth Press.

Cornhill magazine refused an article by her on Scottish author James Boswell's letters, as she complained to Violet in 1905: "Without a word, but a printed slip. . . . I have been writing little articles for Mrs. L. I want to work like a steam engine, though editors wont [sic] take what I write. I must show you what I have done . . . and please dont [sic] say you want to alter heaps of things or I shall give up writing altogether and take to drink, or society."

So Virginia Stephen suffered the inevitable pangs of beginning writers through all time. When Leo Maxse of the *National Review* took her on, followed by Bruce Richmond of the *Times Literary Supplement*, she told Violet in 1905 that this gave her "a little cause for joy in the face of that righteous old

Guardian. Really, I never read such pedantic commonplace as the Guardianese: it takes up the line of a Governess and maiden Lady and high church Parson mixed; how they ever got such a black little goat into their fold, I can't conceive."

The "black little goat" began a long career of writing book reviews and articles for prestigious journals. To Emma Vaughan, aka "Toadlebinks," she wrote in 1905 that "I am realising the ambition of our youth, and actually making money—which, however, I spend long before I make. I am writing for—now for my boast—The Times Lit. Supplement, The Academy, The National Review, The Guardian—Aint [sic] that respectable." She was twenty-three.

Her reviews, especially the earlier ones, show a delight in irony, sometimes at the expense of the writer concerned. Here is part of her review of *A Dark Lantern* by Elizabeth Robins, published in the *Guardian* in May 1905:

> Of this novel it can be said without exaggeration that every page interests. If such a thing were possible, it might almost be added that the interest it excites is not quite of the right quality. Miss Robins has the gift of charging her air with electricity, and her readers wait for the expected explosion in a state of high tension. This is partly due to the fact that she is always in earnest . . . as it is, she is too closely interested in her characters to be able to take a dispassionate view of them. . . . But there can be no doubt that few living novelists are so genuinely gifted as Miss Robins, or can produce work to match hers for strength and sincerity.

I am not sure that any novelist—with due respect to Robins— would have been delighted by this review, protesting, as it does, too much.

In a review of Elizabeth McCracken's *The Women of America*, also published in the *Guardian* in May 1905, she wrote the following:

Miss McCracken, in her investigations into the natural history of the American Woman, travelled over nearly the whole of the United States in a journey which occupied six months, which she found to be too short. . . . Instead of [providing] a scientific treatise on the nature of woman or a blue-book upon her place in the national life, she gives us fourteen snapshots of the woman herself as she works or plays. . . . This method is admittedly superficial, but in the space of one short volume we are taken over a great distance of country and shown many queer people living out-of-the-way lives.

Again, in a review of a book that was evidently fairly forget-table, there comes an ironic tone, covering a youthful naiveté. The slight archness and nervous superiority of a very young reviewer tended to mock the book in question, not very subtly.

The essay as a form was already losing popularity in the early 1900s. But it suited Virginia's particular cast of mind and her way of thinking. After all, she had been reared on great essays, from Montaigne on. In an essay, as in the sort of creative non-fictional piece that is popular again today, you can mix facts, ideas, imagination, wit, and purpose. As she herself wrote in "The Decay of Essay-Writing" in 1905, "Almost all essays be-gin with a capital 'I'—'I think, I feel'—and when you have said that, it is clear that you are not writing history or philosophy or biography or anything but an essay, which may be brilliant or profound, which may deal with the immortality of the soul, or the rheumatism in your left shoulder, but is primarily an expression of personal opinion."

Virginia continued writing essays because she enjoyed the freedom to be personal, even if the *Times Literary Supplement*, the publisher of most of her reviews, initially refused them and wanted straight reviewing. Although Bruce Richmond, the editor from 1902 to 1938, criticized her for what he called her lack of academic spirit, he became her most influential mentor during these years. "I learnt a lot of my craft writing for him; how to compress; how to enliven; & also was made to read with a pen & notebook, seriously."

At *Cornhill* magazine, for which she wrote on the memoirs of Sarah Bernhardt and Dorothy Nevill, on the presidency of Theodore Roosevelt, and on the journal of Lady Holland, she crossed swords too often with the editor, Reginald Smith. "I really believe, dear Miss Stephen, that if you will put heart and head into it, you will make a mark in reviewing." she cited him saying to her. When he refused her short story "Memoirs of a Novelist" in 1909, their association ended.

Virginia learned the hard way, as most writers do. You send things out in haste, forgetting stamps and addresses, and are outraged that you are not taken seriously. Then you pay attention and do the work—or not. The most striking thing for me about the young Virginia Stephen was her capacity for work. She would not give up; she would vent rage or despair in a letter to a friend and then begin again. In 1903, she wrote to Violet, "I always think I might write so much better if I took time or trouble—or something else which I never do take." But during these years she made herself take both time and trouble, and she transformed her own work. She wrote and rewrote, beginning a lifelong attention to the right word and sentence. She argued with editors—she was Leslie Stephen's daughter, after all—but she was aware of what they had to teach her, and she learned from them fast.

An amusing anecdote appears in a letter written to Violet Dickinson in August 1907:

> We went and had tea with Henry James today; and Henry James fixed me with his staring blank eye—it is like a childs [*sic*] marble—and said, "My dear Virginia, they tell me—they tell me—that you—as indeed being your fathers [*sic*] daughter[,] nay your grandfathers [*sic*] grandchild—the descendent I may

say of a century—of a century—of quill pens and ink—ink—ink
pots, yes, yes, yes, they tell me—ahm m m—that you, that you
write in short." This went on in the public street, while we all
waited, as farmers wait for the hen to lay the egg—do they?—
nervous, polite, and now on this foot, now on that. I felt like a
condemned person who sees the knife drop, and stick, and drop
again.

She was not impressed by fame or age, in spite of her own
shyness, and was inclined to be mischievous as a result. This
mixture of sharp observation and deliberate outrageousness
was typical of her, especially when she was young.

From 1909 to 1912 she wrote exclusively for the *Times Literary Supplement*, producing essays that in retrospect show that
she had freed herself from the limited task of a book reviewer
and was writing widely on writers and their life trajectories,
ideas, and influences. Her apprenticeship as a journalist was
at an end. In the essay "Modern Novels," published in 1919,
she laid out her credo on modernism. "The problem before
the novelist at present, as we suppose it to have been in the
past, is to contrive a means of being free to set down what he
chooses. He has to have the courage to say what interests him
is no longer this but that; out of that alone must he construct
his work." Her articles were still anonymous, as was the rule at
the time, but there can have been little doubt for readers about
who wrote the essay. By this time the *Times Literary Supplement* was accepting more or less whatever she sent to it; hers
was an established voice.

4

Looking and Listening

"Looking, looking, looking and making up phrases to match clouds," Virginia Woolf wrote to Vita Sackville-West in 1927. "That is how I travel." As her sister Vanessa sketched habitually, so did Virginia open her eyes and ears, pay attention, and take notes. "My meticulous observations of flowers, clouds, beetles & the price of eggs" is how she ironically referred to her practice in a diary entry in 1918. The habits the sisters formed in early girlhood stayed with them throughout their lives. The letters Virginia wrote to Violet Dickinson from shipboard and from Spain and Portugal, while she was traveling with her brother Adrian, show an attention to detail (which reemerges in her first novel, *The Voyage Out*) that seems to go far beyond simply informing her friend of their whereabouts. A letter to Violet in 1905 describes the boredom of the people she saw on board—"They play the piano all day long and eat sandwiches and drink soup"—and sitting for dinner at the captain's table: "I have to talk to him about twin screws. Would you like to marry a sailor?"

What the critic James Wood has called "serious noticing" was always her forte and her fascination. Virginia walked the streets of London and in the countryside, and she sat at tea tables, noticing. Detail is at the heart of fiction writing, so that the "infinite strange shapes" can be brought to life on the page. In her fiction, especially beginning with *Jacob's Room*, she spun the details into vivid life: the Greek women knitting, the children playing, the plump French women posing on monuments, and the details of the Cornish coast seen from Timmy Durrant's boat as he and Jacob sail around the point of Land's End. There are a thousand instances. It was always crowds, streets, scenes, rooms glimpsed through windows, or life seen as if from a passing train that seized her imagination; she caught the people and the places with an almost cinematic speed. Whether consciously or not, she was of her time: cinema was just beginning, and scientists were suggesting that matter was not the solid thing it seemed.

The ability to seize the detail and stuff of life is perpetually visible in her letters, where Virginia describes what people wore, such as a terrible hat or dress; what they said at parties or at dinners; and also scenes, landscapes, views, furniture, and food. Her description to Katherine Cox in 1912 of her honeymoon to Spain gives a vivid if rather pedestrian picture of herself and Leonard: "At this very moment, Leonard sits on a red plush chair about 6 feet away from me, opposite him my open box with drawers hanging out, and a handsome cupboard by his side, writing the first chapter of his new great work, which is about the suburbs." In the same letter she asked, "Why do you think people make such a fuss about marriage and copulation?" The recipients of her letters must have been surprised, amused, and sometime confused. Life as she saw it was a mixture, a jumble of beauty and scurrilousness, of the trivial and the deeply serious. Her mind and eye could not keep still, and she poured her impressions out daily, for most of her life, to the people she cared for most.

On the way to Lisbon on her first journey abroad, with her brother Adrian, Virginia noted the trees, the flowers, and the weather in Granada, where they stopped, in a kind of exhausted daze. "Think of orange trees, with oranges, and every other kind of tree with large green leaves, and all the blossoms you can think of," she wrote to Violet Dickinson in 1905. "The cottage garden is nothing to it. There, my descriptive faculty is blasted." In one fluid move, she then left behind lists and exactness of description for the kind of evocation of atmosphere that invited the reader to join in: "All the blossoms you can think of." While claiming her own descriptive faculty "blasted," she began in one move to create the kind of sentence that she would be known for later in life. The looking, listening, and experiencing continued, but suddenly the writer has thrown them all to the wind and asked the reader to fill in the gaps.

The wide sweep and bold images of her later fiction, the "fin in the waste of waters," the huge movements of the sun across the sky in *The Waves*, the arbitrary speed of time passing in *To the Lighthouse*, began to appear in her early writing. She knew she was tempted to be slapdash, and editors figuratively rapped her over the knuckles for it; but her own speed of intuition, a rapid way of making a mark in a particular place, as an abstract painter would, became fine-tuned into a faultless technique, her signature style. As Vanessa moved toward more abstract painting under the influence of the postimpressionists, so Virginia, in her fiction at least, came to draw life in impressionistic rapid prose. In her short stories "The Mark on the Wall" and "Kew Gardens" she seemed to glory in the details; they are what create the story. The mark on the wall could be anything and gives rise to all sorts of speculation, but it turns out to be a snail. In her short story "An Unwritten Novel" she extrapolates an entire story from a woman sitting opposite her on a train, rubbing the glass of the window.

Virginia's long association with painters changed her way of seeing. Vanessa and her friends (Duncan Grant, Roger Fry, and the French painter Jacques Raverat), the work of Fry's Omega Workshops, and the influence from France of the postimpressionist movement, all gave her an interest in form that no Victorian novelist could or would have expressed—and not just form, but detail: where to delineate, where to omit, and where to focus. For years she sent her work to Raverat (whom she called the "volatile Frog") and valued his opinion even more than that of her writer friends. He knew form and construction. He knew what to leave out. He could criticize her work with the eye of a painter and the detachment that comes from working in a different art form, as well as from having grown up in a different culture. She had not always appreciated the shock of the new as exhibited at Fry's Omega Workshops in Fitzroy Square. As was true for many others in London at the time, the simplicity and impressionistic sweep of the work, the bright clashing colors, and the sheer oddness of the way the aficionados dressed were too much of a challenge to her eye. But she learned, discovering what she could admire, and during the years of her marriage she often bought plates and furnishings from them. If her expression of her own visual taste was sometimes tentative, when she was with her sister and friends it was nevertheless something she consciously trained herself in. It was not Victorian, and that was what mattered.

But back to the novel. What place has the visual in literature? In a long letter to Clive Bell, from Manorbier in Pembrokeshire in 1908, Virginia wrote, "I think a great deal of my future and settle what book I am to write—how I shall re-form the novel and capture multitudes of things at present fugitive, enclose the whole, and shape infinite strange shapes. I take a good look at woods in the sunset, and fix men who are breaking stones with an intense gaze, meant to sever them from the past and the future—all these excitements last out my walk, but tomorrow I know, I shall be sitting down to the inanimate old phrases."

Virginia often expressed the tension between the new and the old, such as the "semi-transparent envelope or luminous halo" she wrote of in 1919 in "Modern Novels" as a description of life, set against the "row of gig-lamps" set out by three contemporary male novelists: Arnold Bennett, H. G. Wells, and John Galsworthy. Plodding descriptions were out. So was conscientious scene setting. Her work was all light and movement—and this was where she came close, instinctively, to the postimpressionists and modernity in art—and the flicker of human consciousness as it moved over matter and made sense of it.

"Modern Novels" contains both her opposition to the concerns of what she called "materialists" of the novel and her own evolving vision of what fiction could do: "Is it not possible that the accent falls a little differently, that the moment of importance came before or after, that, if one were free and could set down what one chose, there would be no plot, little probability, and a vague general confusion in which the clear-cut features of the tragic, the comic, the passionate, and the lyrical were dissolved beyond the possibility of separate recognition?" The questions arising from her earlier years—what is life, what does it look like and sound like—are aired here in public; but it's almost as if she is still asking herself the question—is it not possible?

Throughout her youth, Virginia walked, looked, listened, and noticed the details: men breaking stones, a bat in the church, other people's hats and mannerisms. She moved all the time between detail, fact, and observation, on the one hand, and broad strokes and evocative images, on the other, the painterly conjuring of "infinite strange shapes" into life on the page. She asked herself the perpetual question: Is it not possible? And if it is, *how* is it possible? How may it be done?

As a painter may observe and draw and then create movement with the sweep of a brush, Virginia wanted both the attention to detail and the uniting whole. In her 1908 letter to Clive, she wrote presciently, "Ah, it is the sea that does it! perpetual movement, and a border of mystery, solving the limits of fields, and silencing their prose." A line of pure poetry, it delineates her own territory: the mystery of the sea, the prose of land—and life, evolving, to be caught in the perpetual movement between the two.

The Place

I went to St. Ives on one of the wettest weekends of the English summer of 2015 and walked up from the old fishing village toward the Victorian end of town, where the Stephen family spent its annual summer holidays until Virginia was thirteen. Leslie Stephen had the long summer vacations of an independent scholar, and he and Julia simply moved their entire household from London to Talland House in Cornwall every summer. Their rented house belonged to the Great Western Railway Company; it sits just above the small railway station, whose track still disappears into the hill on its way to St. Erth, where you change to get the train from Penzance to Paddington.

There are some things that are givens in a writer's life: parents, of course; siblings; position in society; and place. Virginia Stephen grew up in London, at Hyde Park Gate, but her childhood summers were spent at St. Ives, where she and her sister and two brothers ran wild on the immense beaches and were noticed by locals for their eccentric habit of bathing in the sea. Behind the escallonia hedge that still frames Talland House, she watched the beam of the lighthouse sweep around, flooding the land and retreating, every night. It's a great gift, of course, to have long summer holidays beside the sea; it was then, and is now, the privilege of a class that could afford it. The Stephens, like my own great-grandparents, assumed it as a right and a necessity. Generations of English children have played on the beaches of England, with buckets and spades and sand castles, awnings put up against the wind, sandwiches with grit in them, and thermoses of hot tea after cold swims in choppy water.

So, reflecting on the strength and vitality of childhood seaside memories, I went to look for Talland House, which did not appear on any town map. At the St. Ives Visitor Information Centre in the town hall, I asked where the house was.

"You can't go there, you know." The woman at the desk was quite dismissive.

"Why not?"

"It's private. It's been developed. It's private flats now."

"Well, I can look at it from the outside."

"No, you can't, it's all private property."

"Well, I can look at it from a distance."

"You'd have to walk up the Terrace, turn right on Albert Road, and look at it from below, from opposite the hospital. But you won't see much."

With this negative advice spurring me on, I marched uphill, up the long street called the Terrace to its end, where a vast hotel has been built, turned right on Albert Road (past the new hotel and the Edward Hain Hospital), and found myself at the right spot. "You can't go there." Well, of course not. "There" was the nineteenth century. "There" was the Stephen family, all of its members long dead. "There" was a novel that has echoed through my own life for fifty years, even though I was born the year after its author died. I was "there" as much as I could be, a twenty-first century visitor, all her senses sharpened to feel for the essence of the only "there" that was left to me: a house, a place, a view.

Talland House was flanked on one side by new apartments, the sort of glossy, glass-walled, high niches people buy for their sea views, but the gate was left open and I walked up to the house, where nobody was to be seen and the only sign of occupation was an open sash window with a bedcover hanging out of it. The house is square and unlike any other house in town; it has wrought-iron balconies, a porch, and windows with small square mullions set around a central pane. The house was in fairly bad shape, with grass growing in the gutters, its cream paint cracked in places, and its white woodwork green-stained. It stared out at the sea. There was the headland, the island, the Godrevy Light that no longer sends its beam sweeping across land and water but has been replaced by a small ten-second LED on the rock. Radar and GPS have made lighthouses obsolete; but the lighthouse itself, white-painted on the dark rock of its island, is still there.

I stood in the garden and looked. I found several wild strawberries and ate them. I picked a bay leaf and a sprig of honeysuckle. There were roses and big fuchsia bushes growing, and lavender, red-hot-pokers, and hydrangeas. Three lawns descended the hill, diminishing in size and flanked by stone. The view was framed by a shaggy palm on one side and a tall cypress on the other. Someone had cut the grass, but not recently. I don't carry a camera, so I tried a sketch of the house in my notebook—its iron pilasters twisted like kite tails, its balconies, its unusual windows, and its central blind alcove. The house sat for me as I drew, balancing my notebook on my knee in the rain. There were no voices, only the movement of the wind in the trees. More than a hundred years ago the Stephen family made its last voyage here. Virginia and her siblings peered over the hedge, saw the house inhabited by others, and felt the pangs of nostalgia for a family life that had abruptly come to an end.

Coming away from Talland House, I found a path down to the beach that went around the railway line—the path taken, perhaps, by Paul and Minta in *To the Lighthouse* the evening that Mrs. Ramsay sat knitting her sock, to the rocky overhang where Minta lost her grandmother's brooch. You can't know but can only imagine. That novel sits so much more surely in the scenery of St. Ives than it does on the Isle of Skye, where Woolf set it. Landscapes inhabit us, and surface even against our will, as we are writing or reading. We come back again and again to the places of our childhood, to the sounds and smells, the air, the vegetation, and the look of it all. Wherever the novel is ostensibly set, this was the place, as it was also the place where the sun rose, moved across the sky, and set again in *The Waves* and where in *Jacob's Room* the child Jacob went to bed with the sheep's jawbone he had found comfortably within reach.

St. Ives is full of noise: not just the cries of summer vacationers and the shouts of children on a beach, but the constant scream of the gulls, the battering of the wind, and the sound of the sea. It's a town built on fishing—pilchards, especially, and mackerel; as a local man explained to us, the pilchards fed off the effluent from the tin mines, so because Cornish tin is no longer mined, the pilchards have fallen away. I have no idea if this is true. It's also, like St. Malo just across the Channel, a place of enormous tides. At low tide all the boats in the harbor are stranded, tipped on their sides like toys abandoned for the night, their moorings loose. Then the water comes creeping up, and gradually they are all afloat again, fit for action. At low tide on the long beach opposite Talland House, no boats are moored, so the huge stretch of wet sand gleams unmarked, and the sea is pulled back like a shawl to expose land, until it (the sea) is almost out of sight. Children on that beach can run and scream into the wind and feel light as leaves, about to be blown away. The waves run into each other, slipping sideways, uncovering a whole new place—a place for a writer to begin, again and again.

I think of Virginia Stephen, an impressionable girl faced with the wild seas and vast tides of St. Ives; I see Mr. Ramsay setting out too late to reach the lighthouse and the fin rising far out in the waste of waters; I hear the whole movement and music of *The Waves* and remember Clarissa Dalloway's new day, "as if issued to children on a beach."

At Porthminster, the wide beach immediately in front of Talland House, there was nobody at all when I walked back, past the railway station and toward the center of town and the fishing cottage where I was staying. The beach was wet and windswept, the sand gleaming, the sea metallic. On the street, going back, I had to close my umbrella because it threatened to turn inside out. I'd been to the place I wasn't supposed to go to—I imagined the owner telling the people in the Visitor Information Centre not to encourage curious Woolf fans who have come all the way from America, carrying their notebooks and umbrellas—and had eaten its wild strawberries, picked its honeysuckle, and looked for a long time at its view while leaning on a stone wall. As I looked, I thought of the child who became the writer, letting in the huge natural world and its implications: waves, wind, cloud patterns, rocks, sand, and, amid it all, the glory and fragility of being human.

In her 1939 essay "A Sketch of the Past," Virginia wrote the following:

> If life has a base that it stands upon, if it is a bowl that one fills and fills and fills—then my bowl without a doubt stands upon this memory. It is of lying half asleep, half awake, in bed in the nursery at St. Ives. It is of hearing the waves break, one, two, one, two, and sending a splash of water over the beach; and then breaking, one, two, one, two behind a yellow blind. It is of hearing the blind draw its little acorn across the floor as the wind blew the blind out. It is of lying and hearing this splash and seeing this light and feeling, it is almost impossible that I should be here; of feeling the purest ecstasy I can conceive.

This is the original place of childhood, where you experience for the first time the beauty and complexity of the world. It is the place a writer comes back to, consciously and unconsciously, again and again. Marcel Proust made the idea familiar that one memory opens up all the rest. Virginia Stephen, his contemporary and passionate admirer, knew the same thing as the little acorn tapped on the bedroom floor at Talland House, the blind moved, and the waves sounded on the shore.

There is something in the lives of most writers that continually recurs and will not go away: a desire to express an inexpressible feeling, to capture a memory, to go where it leads. This indefinable something, this ur-memory, is, I think, the missing ingredient when we talk of learning how to write. There has to be—doesn't there?—the desire that is almost as old as you are. Without it, everything falls flat in the end. It's bound up with place and the people who were around you in that place, and it may be ecstatic or painful, but it is what marks you as the writer you are—the Brontës' Yorkshire moors, Thomas Hardy's Egdon Heath, Dickens's oppressive blacking factory in the heart of London.

Or it is a memory as evanescent as light coming through leaves. In Pier Paolo Pasolini's great film *Oedipus*, the infant Oedipus lies in the lap of his mother, watching light coming through leaves as she feeds him. The whole life of the man —wandering, killing his father, searching for his mother, blindness—is contained in this moment that begins and ends the film. Virginia Stephen's life began and ended with water, and water sounds through all her novels. It is bigger and more powerful than she is: the small child, safe in bed, listening to the waves on the shore. So place is both actual and metaphorical; one becomes the other; the writer stumbles after images, finding her way. At the end of *The Waves* we discover where she is going, with its last words: "O, Death!"

Leslie Stephen gave up his lease on the house at St. Ives when his wife died and the huge Porthminster Hotel was built, blocking his view of the beach. Virginia was thirteen. She lost her mother and that beloved place all in one year. She could have had no idea that the summer of 1895 would be the last one she and her family would spend there, all together. She came back once as an adult with her brothers and her sister and peered through the escallonia hedge, where they had been happy in another time. It was all still there. But they were in exile, like Oedipus, and they knew it. Much later, in 1921, when staying with friends at Zennor in Cornwall, she wrote to Vanessa, "Ka [Katherine Cox] wants me to lunch with the Millie Drews at Talland—she [Millie] . . . . fears that the associations may be too painful for me." She did not go.

Loss is so often the spur to writing: the lost place, the lost parent, the lost love. It may work its way to the surface years after the loss has occurred, but it lends sharpness and poignancy to the writing. Memory keeps the lost person or place unchanged. Henri Alain-Fournier's *Le Grand Meaulnes*, published in 1913, the same year as Proust's first volume of *À la Recherche du Temps Perdu*, is an early example of such exploration in fiction of place and memory. We go to the enchanted place as children, and then in adult life it is hidden or removed or we can't find it on any map. In writing decades later about Talland House, Virginia Woolf went back to Virginia Stephen's lost place in the world, where her mother, as Mrs. Ramsay, sits on the stone step only to disappear and to be painted years later by Lily Briscoe—to exist forever in the vivid impressionist blur on a canvas that may be stored in an attic unseen, as Lily Briscoe imagines in the last pages of *To the Lighthouse*, but that will nevertheless endure.

6

Family and Friends

When Virginia Stephen wrote rather wistfully to her brother Thoby that talk was surely the best educator, she did not foresee how thoroughly talk—intellectual conversation, as well as argument and gossip—would soon fill her own life. The Stephen children's lives changed radically after their father's death. In November 1904 they moved to 46 Gordon Square in Bloomsbury. Immediately Virginia wrote to Violet Dickinson, "I am feeling really quiet and happy and able to stretch my legs out on the sofa for the first time in 7 months. The house is a dream of loveliness."

Because the atmosphere was relaxed and welcoming and no social niceties had to be observed, Thoby's friends from Cambridge gradually began coming to the house. Nobody had to sit on the furniture; nobody changed for dinner. Among them were future economist John Maynard Keynes, writer and satirist Lytton Strachey, Clive Bell, novelist E. M. Forster, and later, artists Roger Fry and Duncan Grant.

In "Phyllis and Rosamond," a short story written in 1906 in which young women from Kensington visit Bloomsbury, Virginia had already captured the spirit of the era: She had Phyllis theorize that living in Bloomsbury meant that one could grow up as one liked. In the same year, in a letter to Madge Vaughan, with whom she had been staying, she recounted, "We have begun our Bohemian dissipations: tonight Thoby is reading a paper to the Friday Club upon the Decadence of Modern Art."

The first two years in Gordon Square—before the ill-fated expedition to Constantinople (Istanbul) during which both Vanessa and Thoby fell ill (Thoby fatally)—really began what was to be known later as "Bloomsbury." There were the Thursday club meetings to discuss philosophy, and there was Vanessa's Friday club for artists. There were innumerable discussions on all topics, including sexual behavior, since several of Thoby's friends were homosexual and called themselves "the buggers." So marriage, not-marriage, friendship, "buggery," "sapphism," and all stops in between were up for review.

All in their early twenties, the Stephen siblings were extremely serious, as well as casually mocking. Bloomsbury has come to be associated with certain attitudes—snobbery, even anti-Semitism, debauchery, artistic nihilism, and a high-thinking exclusiveness that bore no relation to real life. But what its members were, above all, was young. It's worth remembering that this "humdrum little society, which has but a small orbit or axle or whatever the thing is, to revolve upon," as Virginia described it to Violet in 1906, was the ad hoc arrangement of four young people who found themselves suddenly very much alone and who decided that they were going to set up house together and live differently from the older, Victorian generation. They would get rid of the furniture, both literally and metaphorically. They had the sudden freedom to experiment and the space in which to do it.

Virginia looked back later on the move from Kensington to Bloomsbury when she wrote in her diary that a Kensington writer she was reviewing "makes me consider that the gulf which we crossed between Kensington and Bloomsbury was the gulf between respectable mum[m]ified humbug & life crude and impertinent, perhaps, but living. The breath of South Kensington lives in her pages—almost entirely, I believe, because they would not mention either copulation or w.c.'s [water closets, or bathrooms]."

In 1936 Virginia wrote of the experience of Bloomsbury in a letter to her nephew Julian Bell, then age twenty-eight: "At your age, what with all the family deaths and extreme intensities . . . I felt I had lived through all the emotions and wanted only peace and loneliness. All the horrors of life had been pressed against our eyes, so very crude and raw. And then there came a burst of splendour, those two years at Gordon Square before Thoby died, a kind of Elizabethan renaissance, much though I disliked the airs that young Cambridge gave itself."

All the proposals of marriage she received in her twenties came from this group of young Bloomsbury men, including Lytton Strachey, who openly preferred his own sex. Leonard Woolf, who had disappeared after graduation into the civil service in Ceylon (Sri Lanka) and did not come back till 1911, was also one of Thoby's Cambridge friends. Virginia was fascinated by their talk and their apparent worldliness, but she also compared herself critically to them. In 1905 she wrote to Violet, "No one really takes very much interest, why should they, in my scribblings. Do you think I shall ever write a really good book?" Later, she would ask both Clive Bell and Lytton Strachey the same question. She would, in the end, be taken seriously by both of them.

Meanwhile, life at Gordon Square went on in its simultaneously chaotic and densely organized way. "We were full of experiments and reforms. We were going to do without table napkins . . . we were going to paint; to write; to have coffee after dinner instead of tea at nine o'clock." Thoby and Vanessa set up their clubs for discussions. New members came by and joined in: Augustus John's painter friend Henry Lamb, Henry's brother Walter, Gwen Darwin (Charles Darwin's granddaughter), Ka Cox (who fell in love with the poet Rupert Brooke), and Marjorie Strachey (Lytton's sister). Vanessa's painter friends imposed their arguments, French impressionist versus traditional British, on the writers in the group.

As a result Virginia began thinking seriously about painting —not about doing it, but about the discipline of it, the imagery, and the techniques. She went to the James McNeill Whistler exhibition in the New Gallery on Regent Street in February 1905 and was impressed, but she criticized the George Frederick Watts memorial exhibition at the Royal Academy, in contrast. She admired the paintings of Walter Sickert. In 1903 she began to refer to her diary as a sketchbook. In her novels—particularly in *To the Lighthouse*, in which Lily Briscoe tries and fails and then finally succeeds in finishing her painting—Virginia used painting and painters' imagery. She commented, always a little nervously, on her sister's paintings. When she began a long correspondence with the French painter Jacques Raverat, who married her friend Gwen Darwin, the explicit links between writing and painting in her mind were evident.

After Thoby's death in November 1906, the first chapter of Bloomsbury was at an end. Vanessa married her suitor, Clive Bell, and Virginia and her younger brother, Adrian, were left alone. They moved to a house in Fitzroy Square not far away. With the evenings of discussion and intense sociability at an end, Virginia retreated into reading, her own writing, and a teaching job at Morley College that brought her some income as well as contact with people and social classes other than her own. That Vanessa had accepted Clive's proposal just two days after Thoby's death upset Virginia deeply: she had lost not only a brother but a sister, too. The family was dissolved; the Cambridge fraternity had all moved on; she was now twenty-five and felt newly abandoned. She wrote to Violet in December

1906, "I shall want all my sweetness to gild Nessa's happiness. It does seem strange and intolerable sometimes." In her next letter to Violet that month she wrote, "The world is full of kindness and stupidity. I wish everyone didn't tell me to marry. Is it crude human nature breaking out?" About her brothers, she wrote to Madge Vaughan in 1907, "It is very hard not to have him [Thoby] here. Adrian is well—but I can't be a brother to him!"

There is a subdued loneliness in Virginia's letters to her friends at this time and, with the felt loss of her sister, who had been there all her life, an undercurrent of her need for them. She confided to Violet in 1907, "Nessa still writes very inarticulate letters. I dont [sic] much realise what has happened. Still, it would have been unbearable if she hadn't married. I dont [sic] get reconciled to anything. The thought of you makes a considerable difference: do you see that written out letter for letter?"

So the talk had ended, for the time being. The uproarious evenings of argument, coffee and wine drinking, confessions, and obsessions at Gordon Square were over. But by March 1907 Virginia was writing enthusiastically to her brother-in-law, Clive Bell, about an argument she had had about Vanessa on a visit to Cambridge with an older admirer, Walter Headlam. Gradually, over the next few years, she approached Clive—first as a way of getting closer to her sister, then as a confidant about her writing, and eventually as a man she was openly flirting with, especially after Vanessa had given birth to her first child, Julian. They all went to Cornwall for a vacation together in 1908, and she and Clive ganged up on Vanessa for her domesticity and baby worship. The "talk" was resolutely intellectual and combative.

Throughout 1908, Virginia's letters show her longing for Vanessa—she calls her "Beloved" and "Honey-bee"—and her increasing dependence on Clive, for both input on her novel and personal compliments. That year she went to Paris and Italy with Adrian and wrote to Lytton Strachey, "We had very successful travels . . . and mild Bohemian society. We drank an immense amount of coffee and sat out under the electric light talking about art. I wish we were 10 years younger, or 20 years older, and could settle to our brandy and cultivate the senses."

Even given that the letter was written to the worldly Lytton, there is a change of tone. Perhaps with Clive and Lytton she did not allow herself the complaints and slight wistfulness that she expressed when writing to her female friends. Yet here the spirit of Bloomsbury seems to have asserted itself again in Virginia. Friends came to visit once the two siblings were back in Fitzroy Square. "We had Lytton last night," she wrote to Clive in 1908. "You will be glad to hear that I am not in love with him, nor is there any sign that he is in love with me. Then Duncan Grant came; we had a very desultory talk. DG is difficult, but charming." She also became aware that Adrian had had a love affair with Grant, who would later become her sister's lover and the father of her daughter, Angelica.

Thus Bloomsbury had led not only to art and writing but also to intellectual fervor, sexual entanglements, lifelong friendships, and much gossip, which Virginia loved. It was the platform for the next stage of her apprenticeship. She had to deal with the patronizing, often sexist attitudes of upper-class, educated young men; with living with her siblings; with earning her own money; with the dissolution of both her real family and her chosen family; and with her own eventual loneliness. By 1911 she was sufficiently secure in herself to move away from Adrian into the house she called Little Talland House, at Firle in Sussex, giving it the name of the beloved house in Cornwall that had been lost to them all. That year she wrote to Vanessa,

"It's odd, retiring from the world like this. I feel as if I were 15 again[;] one begins to think of books and describing scenery just as one used [to do]. I am reading *Les Liaisons Dangereuses* with great delight."

. . . .

Family is a writer's first society; friends come next. What we notice about other people and what we feel for them are the wellspring of fiction writing. There is no novel without characters and no character without failings, hopes, and contradictions. Her own family and the extended family of Bloomsbury were Virginia Stephen's palette and foundation for experiment. She was endlessly fascinated by human behavior and endlessly drawn to people. Friends reported how she sometimes questioned them as if conducting interviews, on everything from politics to dress to sexual habits. She was never a hermit, except during the long solitary walks on the Downs that she began taking when she moved to Sussex. Throughout her life she wanted people, sociability, and talk; then there would be the long walk of introspection, during which her characters began to speak to her in their turn.

Balancing one's time is always a challenge for a writer: How much life, how much work? For Virginia Stephen, born into a crowded household—one of four siblings and three half siblings, always part of a whole—solitude was something to be fought for and prized. But there was always the need, too, for the fertilizing relationship, the person glimpsed in a crowd, the expectation of a friend coming to tea. There was the delight of talk and then its surfeit. She always experienced the conflict, whether in London or in the country, of quiet days with Leonard versus the fizz of parties and society, of talk or silence. She apprenticed herself to both to create the equilibrium she needed—then it escaped her, again and again, and vivaciousness gave way to exhaustion, excitement to a wasteland of dreariness.

In 1917, when she had been married to Leonard Woolf for five years, she wrote in her diary, "I was glad to come home & feel my real life coming back again—I mean life here with L. Solitary is not quite the right word; one's personality seems to echo out across space, when he's not there to enclose all one's vibrations. This is not very intelligibly written; but the feeling itself is a strange one—as if marriage were a completing of the instrument, & the sound of one alone penetrates as if it were a violin robbed of its orchestra or piano."

I think this a wonderful statement, both about marriage and about a writer's need for solitude as well as closeness. The solo violin needs its orchestra, too.

Routine

The very word *routine* may sound off-putting to the beginning writer. (Isn't *inspiration* more important?) But we don't get very far without discipline (an even worse word) and a certain amount of routine—what successful writers call showing up at the page.

Virginia Stephen was no stranger to routine in life. A Victorian household depended on it: the routines of getting up and going to bed, family mealtimes, instructing servants what to cook, receiving guests, and visiting in turn. But it was the kind of routine—like her own mother's routine of visiting the poor and the sick—that could destroy a writer's life, or at least gobble it up. Her father's routine was to shut people out of his study and read into the wee hours of the night. But he was a man; he benefited from the routine tasks performed by women and servants.

Virginia would have to invent her own routines, as would Vanessa, who had to take over the running of 22 Hyde Park Gate after their mother's and Stella's deaths. Resentment about the role that men traditionally allotted to women continued throughout both of the Stephen girls' lives. All those teas, dinners, polite drawing-room attendances, and obligations to listen to men, both young and old! In 1907 she wrote to Violet Dickinson about an elderly man who asked her what several great writers had said when they came to dinner with her father. "The astonishing thing is that these great people always talked much as you and I talk; Tennyson, for instance, would say to me, 'Pass the salt' or, 'Thank you for the butter.'"

The routines established in Virginia's girlhood—lessons in the morning, walking in the afternoon (around and around Kensington Gardens, in all kinds of weather, with her father), reading, and diary and letter writing after tea—continued throughout her teenage and adult life. They later became the basis of her life with Leonard, who grew almost more addicted to them than she did. In 1914, after her breakdown a year earlier, before he went on a brief trip he made her sign a contract for a routine that included drinking milk and going to bed early, but not writing. Routine, he and her doctors agreed, was essential for someone with her temperament and history. This regimen included an incredibly bland diet that made her put on weight.

Although the social routines of Virginia's youth were quite different, they too were imposed by others. In the early days of her adolescence, especially when the Duckworth brothers, George and Gerald, were still living at Hyde Park Gate, there was the regular obligation to go out into society and practice its manners. The "London season" still exercised its demands on marriageable young women.

In 1901, at age nineteen, Virginia wrote the following to her friend Emma Vaughan:

Our London season, about which you ask, was of the dullest description. I only went to three dances—and I think nothing else. But the truth of it is, as we frequently tell each other, we are failures. Really, we can't shine in Society. I don't know how it's done. We aint [sic] popular, we sit in corners and look like mutes who are longing for a funeral. However, there are more important things in this life—from all I hear, I shant [sic] be asked to dance in the next, and that is one of the reasons why I hope to go there.

After their father's death, no longer under the wings of their worldly half brothers the Duckworths, Vanessa and Virginia happily gave up any attempt to "shine in Society." They made their own society, and it came to them. The chosen routines of writing, reading, and letter writing for Virginia and painting for Vanessa could expand and fill their lives. There is all the difference in the world between a routine one chooses oneself and one enforced by other people. In her 1917 short story "The Mark on the Wall" she wrote caustically, "Generalisations bring back . . . Sunday in London, Sunday afternoon walks, Sunday luncheons, and also ways of speaking of the dead, clothes, and habits—like the habit of sitting all together in a room until a certain hour, although nobody liked it." You can hear and feel the staleness of Victorian habits and rules of behavior, imagine the clutter and the heavy furniture that the Stephen girls had vowed to get rid of forever.

Left to her own devices, Virginia chose the occasional risky adventure. There was the *Dreadnought* hoax, when Virginia, Vanessa, and their friends dressed up as the Abyssinian royal family and somehow managed to be welcomed aboard the Royal Navy battleship HMS *Dreadnought*. Escapades like this were the very opposite of Victorian propriety. Leonard tended to set himself up as the antidote to such adventures, as their marriage went on. But she knew what she had gained from marrying him; decades later, when the sisters had been discussing their marriages, Vanessa told her son Julian that Virginia found Leonard absolutely dependable and like a rock, which was what she badly wanted. From the point of view of Virginia's apprenticeship to a writer's life, she was drawn to his immense self-discipline, his steadiness, and his appreciation of her work. There is always a risk in marriage, and Virginia spelled out her misgivings in a very frank letter to Leonard in May 1912, just before she accepted his third proposal, naming his "foreignness" as a Jew, her instability, her lack of physical feeling for him, and her need for independence—but ending with the words, "We both of us want a marriage that is a tremendous living thing, always alive, always hot, not dead and easy in parts as most marriages are. We ask a great deal of life, don't we? Perhaps we shall get it; then, how splendid!"

The fact, which Virginia intuited in this letter, was that her marriage was a solid structure within which she could do her best work. In July 1912 she wrote to Violet Dickinson, "We're both writing hard; he has some journalism to do, and my novel is at last dying. O how sad when it's done! I think some of its [sic] very, or rather, amusing; and as it gets shoved out of my head, another begins; but next year I must have a child." The children she wanted never came and so never interrupted her flow of writing. Leonard made a conscious decision not to have a child, because he thought it would have been too hard on her both physically and mentally. She never quite forgave him for it. The books never made up for her lack of children; books generally do not, although people who don't write them are fond of saying they do. But she was left with all her time to write, without the profound upset to an ordered writing regimen that children inevitably create.

Thus the routines put in place during her childhood at Hyde Park Gate continued with very little change throughout her adult life: reading, writing, walking, letter writing, journal writing, and talk. In 1911 she wrote to Vanessa from Firle while working on the manuscript "Melymbrosia" (which became the novel *The Voyage Out*): "I write all the morning, walk all the afternoon, and read and write and look out of the window the rest of the time." Well into her marriage to Leonard, she wrote in her diary, "Happiness—what, I wonder[,] constitutes happiness? I daresay the most important element is work, & that rarely fails either of us now."

Too often the chaos and upset of mental illness blew this happy routine apart, and then, as her mind speeded into excess, she had the invalid's rigid routines laid upon her once again: the months of bed rest and bland diets; the nonreading, nonwriting life that Charlotte Perkins Gilman, the author of "The Yellow Wall-Paper," described so unforgettably on the American side of the Atlantic. Gilman's short story was published in 1892, and I have not been able to discover whether Virginia had read its scathing indictment of its protagonist's forced isolation and bed rest. Virginia described her own treatment to Vanessa, writing from a nursing home in Twickenham in 1910 about "all the eating and drinking and being shut up in the dark" and warning that "I shall soon have to jump out of a window."

For Virginia Stephen, routine was something to be used yet also to be rebelled against; she knew she needed it, but she also raged against its constraints. The constraints imposed by others always chafed: her own well-established sense of routine, or the rhythm of her days, needed no rules and regulations. When the doctors, Leonard, or the well-meaning religious-minded ladies of the Twickenham home tried to impose their rules, she reacted like a wild horse shut in a stall.

8

"That Dangerous Ground"

Virginia Stephen, having become Virginia Woolf, described her decision to write her first two novels as an effort not to enter "that dangerous ground." That "ground" was the death of her mother in 1895 followed by the death of her half sister two years later, then the death of her father in 1904 followed by the death of her brother Thoby two years after that. Today these events would probably make even the most determined fiction writer turn to memoir to deal with loss and mourning. Virginia Stephen turned in another direction: she set her first novel on a ship and a foreign continent; her second novel revolved around a marriage plot, among a worldly set of people in central London.

Woolf always worked to get rid of the "I" in her fiction, the deadly imposition of the ego that she glimpsed in other writers such as James Joyce, Henry James, and Dorothy Richardson. Yet the house in St. Ives and the long beaches of her childhood there had as much impact on her as the rather gloomy house in London where she lived as a girl in the winter. Those summer days contained all the insouciance of being young and careless: Jacob waking in his bedroom in *Jacob's Room*; the young people going down to the beach in the evening in *To the Lighthouse*; the new day issued to Clarissa Dalloway even in central London; the sun rising over the sea in *The Waves* and its eventual setting. Then there came the deaths: of Percival in *The Waves*; of Mrs. Ramsay in *To the Lighthouse*; of Jacob in *Jacob's*

Room. In these fictional deaths Virginia also anticipated her own death.

Thus the shocks and losses of her own early life emerged transformed in her later books. I think that at some level Virginia protected herself by letting this happen in her maturity, not any earlier. We, as fiction writers, don't exactly choose our topics, but we try to; we want to imagine we are in control, even as we plunge in. The dangerous terrain waits, perhaps, for us to have the ability and skill to cross it. Was it necessary for her as a writer to have suffered all this loss? An Aristotelian view—his notion of potentiality preceding actuality—might suggest that everything that happens to a writer goes to create his or her own genius, as the acorn buried but watered becomes the oak. In the acorn of Virginia Stephen, playing on the beach, perhaps there was always the oak tree of her mature writing. It's one way of looking at a life.

There would be no religious consolation, anyway, for the orphaned and then depleted Stephen children. They had been brought up as humanist atheists, and Thoby had even inscribed in a book he had given to Virginia, "There is no God." Virginia, Vanessa, and Adrian had to draw on reserves of psychological strength and stoicism after the tragedy of Thoby's death from typhoid. They carried on as best they could. But as Hermione Lee has pointed out in her fine biography, "The death intensified her sense of life as a threatened narrow strip between two great grindstones." As a result, the novels she would write would nearly all be elegiac.

The "dangerous ground" was also that of madness—the term being a shorthand for whatever the mental affliction was that tormented her off and on all her life. Her family used the word *mad* easily, in the way of the time, in which mental illness was both more mystifying and less treatable than it is now. Virginia's first breakdown happened just after her mother's death, when she was thirteen. Another followed her father's death, and another her marriage to Leonard Woolf. How did she treat these periodic collapses in her fiction? How did she learn to write about the dangerous ground?

At about the same time that her second novel, *Night and Day*, was published, she wrote "An Unwritten Novel," a short story in which she glimpsed the possibilities of the fluid, speeded-up prose she would use in her later novels. It was a turning point, away from realism. When she wrote to her friend Ethel Smyth in 1930, looking back on that time, she realized that this new piece of writing had some connection with her altered mental states:

> After being ill and suffering every form and variety of nightmare and extravagant intensity of perception—for I used to make up poems, stories and to me inspired phrases all day long as I lay in bed, and thus sketched, I think, all that I now, by the light of reason, try to put into prose—after all this, when I came to, I was so tremblingly afraid of my own insanity that I wrote *Night and Day* mainly to prove to my own satisfaction that I could keep entirely off that dangerous ground. Bad as the book is, it composed my mind. . . . I shall never forget the day I wrote The Mark on the Wall—all in a flash, as if flying, after being kept stone-breaking for months . . . The Unwritten Novel was the great discovery, however. That—again, in one second—showed me how I could embody all my deposit of experience in a shape that fitted it—not that I have ever reached that end; but anyhow I saw, branching out of the tunnel I made, when I discovered that method of approach, Jacobs Room, Mrs. Dalloway etc.—How I trembled with excitement, and then Leonard came in, and I drank my milk, and concealed my excitement, and wrote I suppose another page of that interminable *Night and Day* (which some say is my best book).

The realization that the "dangerous ground" lay close to the sources of her writing came after the fact, perhaps, but that she increasingly risked it, going closer and closer to the material of her life and her mental states, shows a fearlessness in the face of her own demons that I think comes close to explaining how she became the writer she was. She dared to face down her deepest fears. She began to confront them in the last pages of *The Voyage Out*, in which Rachel Vinrace unaccountably (in terms of the novel) falls ill and dies. In Rachel's delirium, the image of the acorn at the end of the blind, which so consoled the young Virginia in her bedroom at Talland House, reappears in a different guise: "Turning her eyes to the window, she was not reassured by what she saw there. The movement of the blind as it filled with air and blew slowly out, drawing the cord with a little trailing sound along the floor, seemed to her terrifying, as if it were the movement of an animal in the room."

The penultimate chapter of the novel reads like a nightmare with its hallucinations and panic. Rachel dreams in her fevered state of " little deformed women sitting under archways, playing cards while the bricks of which the wall was made oozed with damp." The experience of the author's own mental illness is conflated here with the appalling arbitrariness of Thoby's death, as the narrative moves from Rachel's own experience to that of her lover, Terence, who helplessly watches her die. "Thought had ceased, life had come to a standstill." Not only does he feel anguished, stuck at her deathbed, but "he had never been so bored since he was shut up in the nursery alone as a child." That statement carries a raw and even shocking truth: boredom as a response to suffering.

When Virginia wrote *Jacob's Room*, she admitted none of these complex feelings. Jacob is there and then not-there, in a brief concluding paragraph. His room is empty, and only his things remain. The only question left is, what to do with his shoes? The shock felt by the reader as a result of this almost brutal understatement is of a quite different order—the ending is inevitable, though unforeseen. Jacob is one of the millions of young men gone to the Great War, never to return; we see that this has been coming for him all along, although his creator kept us all through the book in the present vivacity of his young life.

In *Mrs. Dalloway* Woolf made this war the source of Septimus Smith's recurrent mental illness. In creating him as a shell-shocked ex-soldier, she grounded and made a place in society and even in history for her own experiences. By fiercely criticizing the methods of his doctors, in scenes based on her own visits to fashionable specialists on Harley Street, she showed their totally inadequate understanding of the extreme pain of mental illness. Septimus's post-traumatic stress disorder (PTSD), as we would call it now, gave her an opportunity to examine fully the twists and turns, the terrors and hallucinations of mental illness as a fact in lives other than her own. (When I first read *Mrs. Dalloway*, when I was young, I thought it was all about a woman giving a party; reading it again, I discovered a novel about PTSD.) The horrors Septimus experiences are incomprehensible and even invisible to everyone else in the novel; but they were well-known to its author.

The courage required for seizing the power of imagination that lives close to insanity is considerable. Virginia Woolf peered into the abyss when she dared to write these scenes and those toward the end of *The Voyage Out*. She worked at the edge, and she knew it.

The First Novel

Virginia Stephen knew that she would be a novelist, not, as her father had projected, a historian, and not simply or solely a reviewer of books. But what kind of novelist? What was to be done with the legacy of the Victorians—the stodgy, prosy plod-dings, as she saw it, of Henry James, Thomas Hardy, George Meredith, and even writers she admired? There had to be a new way, a way through.

Virginia considered poetry and realism as two instincts that refused to combine. It was the old conflict again, the sea and the fields and the shifting liminal place in between. In her first novel, *The Voyage Out*, which took her so many years to write, the wild jungle is set against the petty rules and habits of the travelers, and even though they have traveled so far, civilization is within reach. "It was this sea that flowed up to the mouth of the Thames; and the Thames washed the roots of the City of London." The sea connects the safety of London with the wild-ness of South America and seems to wash between the charac-ters and set them adrift. The booming of the sea is audible all through this first novel.

Virginia's prose style in this first book is, however, far from the fluidity of *Jacob's Room*, *The Waves*, or *Mrs. Dalloway*. She wrote to Violet Dickinson in the summer of 1907, "I shall be miserable, or happy; a wordy sentimental creature or a writer of such English as shall burn the pages." She knew instinctive-ly where she wanted to go—but how would she get there? A few weeks later she wrote again to Violet, "A narrative should be as straight and flexible as the line you stretch between pear trees with your linen on drying" and "If only my flights were longer and less variable I should make solid blocks of sentences, carven and wrought from pure marble; or the Greek marble which absorbs colours." To Nelly, Lady Robert Cecil, she wrote a month later, "I feel like one rolled at the bottom of a green flood, smoothed, obliterated, how should my pockets be full of words?" Apart from strangely predicting her own death, with pockets that would be full not of words but of stones, the question expresses all the anxiety of a writer grappling with subjects as yet too big for her. She had to decide not only whether a narrative could ever be a washing line, or sentences blocks of marble, but also how to write the novels she longed to write while avoiding the major themes of her own life.

Should you write what you know or what you don't know? Virginia Woolf took all the characters in her first book off to South America, a place she had never visited, and put them down in a jungle, where her heroine, Rachel, caught a mysterious disease and died of it. Death crept in, as if in spite of her, and it came just as Rachel had achieved happiness in love. Yet the real impact of the ravages that had happened to Woolf's own family since those first idyllic days at St. Ives would take decades to emerge in her fiction.

Virginia Stephen's first mention of a novel, a manuscript she called "Melymbrosia" (which became *The Voyage Out*) was in 1907. "My writing makes me tremble," she wrote to Violet that October. "It seems so likely that it will be d—d bad—or only slight. This isn't a catch for compliments." Gradually, Clive Bell and Lytton Strachey became her confidants during 1908; perhaps she trusted that they would be more likely to tell her the truth. To Clive she wrote in April 1908, "I dreamt last night that I was showing father the manuscript of my novel; and he snorted, and dropped it on to a table, and I was very melancholy, and read it this morning, and thought it bad." So Leslie Stephen operated on his daughter even after he was dead.

"It comes over me that I know nothing of the art; but blunder in a rash way after motive, and human character; and that I suppose is the uncritical British method; for I should choose my writing to be judged as a chiselled block, unconnected with my hand entirely." Here is the monumental marble block again, the solid unchanging thing.

The interruptions and intrusions were not only internal. In August 1908 she wrote to Vanessa from Wells, in Somerset, where she had gone to work on the novel: "O I have been so peevish all day! I balanced one table on another, and put my writing book on top, and stood on a mound of cushions and tried to write Melymbrosia. But a violin began 2 doors off, and all the tradesmen called, and they came and bashed the floor over my head." She then adds, "I spent a whole hour reading my 100 pages, and came to the conclusion that there is something of a structure in it; I did mean something."

Later that month she was able to write to Clive, "Ah well!—I am in a mood today to care very little what anybody says about Melymbrosia. The mood has lasted indeed seven days. . . . I am aware that the only thing that matters is a thing you cant [sic] control, nor I neither. (I think it should be 'either.')"

In 1911, after three years during which she had been busy writing (articles, letters, and reviews), flirting with admirers, fending off proposals of marriage, moving house, being ill, and visiting friends and having them visit her, she told Clive, "Yesterday I finished the 8th chapter of Mel[ymbrosia]: which brings them [the characters] within sight of the South American shore. That is a third of the book done, I think. From sheer cowardice I didn't bring the other chapters here [to Little Talland House, at Firle in Sussex]. If I thought, 'There, thats [*sic*] solid and done with,' I'm sure I should have the palsy."

By the end of the summer of 1911, Leonard Woolf, her brother Thoby's old friend, was back in England from Ceylon, and by early December he was a tenant of Virginia and Adrian Stephen at 38 Brunswick Square. He proposed to Virginia in May 1912, and she accepted. The first mention of her novel after these events was to Violet on May 22, 1912: "Every morning I write 500 words of The Voyage Out and have already passed my natural limit, but must go on for another 5 chapters." In June she wrote to all her friends to say that she had accepted Leonard's proposal, and she told Madge Vaughan that "he is far and away the most interesting man I know." To Violet she wrote, "By the way, my novel is getting on, in spite of interruptions, and L. wants me to say that if I cease to write when married, I shall be divorced." She told Nelly, Lady Robert Cecil, "He has written a novel, so have I; we both hope to publish them in the autumn."

Thus the long struggle to finish her first novel ended with that calm announcement. She had been through all the doubts and fears of beginning writers; she had plagued her friends with them and begged them for insights on the book and on her writing; and she had written and rewritten, as she struggled with other aspects of her life at the same time. The novel had taken many years to come to its present form, but she, and it, had come through. *The Voyage Out* was published by Gerald Duckworth. This must have felt like a strange arrangement, at some level; but he was the only publisher she thought that she, as a beginner, could call upon, and so she did.

I'm not suggesting that when she met Leonard Woolf, everything was solved—far from it. But she now had a book coming out, a place in life, and a person to care for her, a man who said he would divorce her if she stopped writing. It must have answered many of the questions she had been struggling with. The whole business of writing her books became much calmer. Her husband was a writer, too, so they would write together and read together; it was the basis for their shared life. After they had both published with traditional publishers, Leonard came up with the idea of founding an independent press. It would eventually become the Hogarth Press, named after Hogarth House, their home in Richmond. It freed her at a stroke from the Duckworths (whom the novelist Anthony Powell, who worked for them briefly, described as completely uninterested in literature), and it allowed her and Leonard to publish some of the most avant-garde writers of their time. When they finally were about to publish their own books, she could say at last, and with justification, "I'm the only woman in England free to write what I like. The others must be thinking of series & editors."

The "series and editors" would demand certain restrictions and expect certain conventions. With the Hogarth Press, she could proceed with confidence to write her masterpieces, beginning with *Jacob's Room*. But even then, she wrote to Roger Fry in 1925 just before its publication, "I'll send you my book when it's out—but it is too much of an experiment to be a success." The habit of self-doubt was hard to break.

Virginia Stephen's long apprenticeship to the novel went through various stages, veering from optimism and excitement to despair and back again, a cycle that will be familiar to anyone who writes fiction. She did not get over the tendency to go to extremes of doubt and hope about her novels—does one ever? But at least, having written and published one novel, *The Voyage Out*, she could go on more calmly to write the next, which would be *Night and Day*. When her second novel was published by the Duckworths in 1919, she almost wished that they had turned it down, because she would have liked to publish it independently.

The fear of failure haunted Virginia all her life, but she went on working. It may seem extraordinary to readers today to discover how very uncertain of herself she often was; this great mind, the mind of a genius, went through all the stages that any writer ever does. But at the same time she had her vision. She knew where she wanted to go. She would not go back to a traditional structure. Nor would she ever shirk the complexity and control she had imposed on herself with her method.

"The Mark on the Wall" was prescient of her later fiction and would lead her to the groundbreaking technique she knew was uniquely her own. The story hints at the rhythms of her mature novels:

> Why, if one wants to compare life to anything, one must liken it to being blown through the Tube at fifty miles an hour— landing at the other end without a single hairpin in one's hair! Shot out at the feet of God entirely naked! Tumbling head over heels in the asphodel meadows like brown paper parcels pitched down a shoot [chute] in the post office! With one's hair flying back like the tail of a racehorse. Yes, that seems to express the rapidity of life, the perpetual waste and repair; all so casual, so haphazard . . . But after life. The slow pulling down of thick green stalks so that the cup of the flower, as it turns over, deluges one with purple and red light. Why, after all, should one not be born there as one is born here, helpless, speechless, unable to focus one's eyesight, groping at the roots of the grass, at the toes of Giants?

The daring of Woolf's prose begins to show here. It is also evident in the long slow buildup of the first part of *To the Lighthouse*, in which Mrs. Ramsey sits and cogitates for so long that she forgets she isn't supposed to move, since she's sitting for Lily Briscoe's painting, then the abrupt caesura of the "Time Passes" section and the slow return to the postwar scene in which everything has changed because Mrs. Ramsey is no longer there. Other examples are the controlled counterpoint between the Clarissa Dalloway and Septimus Smith stories in *Mrs. Dalloway* and the regular breathlike rhythm and then acceleration of *The Waves*.

In 1927, in a long letter to Vita Sackville-West, Virginia wrote the following:

> Style is a very simple matter; it is all rhythm. Once you get that, you can't use the wrong words. But on the other hand, here I am sitting after half the morning, crammed with ideas and visions and so on, and can't dislodge them, for lack of the right rhythm. Now this is very profound, what rhythm is, and goes far deeper than words. A sight, an emotion creates this wave in the mind long before it makes words to fit it, and in writing (such is my present belief) one has to recapture this and set this working (which has nothing apparently to do with words) and then as it breaks and tumbles in the mind, it makes words to fit it: But no doubt I shall think differently next year.

There is no fixed blueprint; there is no netting her method once and for all ("No doubt I shall think differently next year"). The reader has to catch her on the wing. But I think this letter shows what Woolf was aiming for, what she was training herself to focus on: a target that was perpetually on the move. So often, reading her, one has the sensation of her running after her vision, throwing her nets across the page to catch what she sees as it flies. It's not until the last paragraph of *The Waves* that she enunciates this rush to capture what she sees; but it's present in her journal and her letters, too. Life rushes past you, and you catch it as you can: the bright and dark vision runs on, always just ahead, always tantalizingly just out of reach.

With one's first novel finished, the writer at least knows that it's possible to do it again. The distance has been covered, and the structure holds. Even so, the writer almost always wants to do it differently. It took Virginia Stephen from her adolescence to her maturity to finish her first full-length work of fiction. The book itself went through so many transformations that its final version looks nothing like its first draft. *The Voyage Out* launched her—but not in the way she wanted to go. *Night and Day*, her second novel —taking place in the streets and drawing rooms of London and delivering its rather scandalous message about friendship, love, and marriage—was much closer to her own social life. But even this novel doesn't come close to the vision she saw ahead of her. The early works of a novelist are often terrains on which to let language and plot out for exercise; they are hints of what may be to come. They also make plain the gap between the original idea and the finished work—the fine Platonic ideal often contrasting in a humiliating way with what is possible and what can be published. If politics is the art of the possible, then so is fiction. The spirit strains for the ideal, the vision glimpsed in a moment of inspiration. But the hard work of getting words on the page, and out into the world, remains.

10

"The Only Woman in England"

When Virginia's books began to be published by the Hogarth Press, as noted in the previous chapter, she told herself gleefully, "I'm the only woman in England free to write what I like." The gap between what she imagined and what was possible was beginning to shrink. The need to please her half brothers at Duckworth Press was over. The need to please and impress readers and critics had not vanished—far from it, but at least she knew that from *Jacob's Room* on, her novels would be published as she wrote them. For any writer this is an immense freedom. Every writer needs a publisher who believes in him or her. It opens the door for the next book, and the next.

So when Woolf wrote in her diary in July 1922, "There's no doubt in my mind that I have found out how to begin (at 40) to say something in my own voice," her apprenticeship was at an end. There would always be the anxiety, the effort to stay true to that voice and follow it to its end, but she had her own method now, as well as the freedom to publish whatever she wrote. She finished *Jacob's Room* and moved straight on to *Mrs. Dalloway*. In September 1922 she wrote in her diary, "My proofs come every day and I could depress myself adequately if I went into that. . . . The thing now reads thin and pointless. . . . I expect to be told I've written a graceful fantasy without much bearing on real life. . . . Anyhow, nature obligingly supplies me with the illusion that I am about to write something good, something rich and deep and fluent, and hard as nails, while bright as diamonds."

In February of that year, she had written, "A mildly unfavorable review of Monday or Tuesday, reported by Leonard from the *Dial* . . . it seems as if I succeed nowhere. Yet, I'm glad to find, I have acquired a little philosophy. It amounts to a sense of freedom. I write what I like writing and there's an end on it."

She had found not only a solid basis in life for her work's publication but also a way of thinking that anticipated negative criticism and defied it. The inner voice, as imposed on Lily Briscoe in *To the Lighthouse* ("Women can't write, women can't paint"), the self-doubt sown in her early in life, did not disappear. But there is nothing like success to build self-confidence and chase away feelings of inferiority, and at last she was beginning to succeed. The times were with her: modernism flourished after the major changes that came as a result of World War I. She felt strongly that any book written or published as if that war had not occurred was a lesser work. The sense that nostalgia or escapism was not possible anymore began to obsess her during this war, as it would more strongly in the early days of World War II, in which she and Leonard (who was Jewish) felt much more directly threatened than they were even by the bombing raids on London in 1917.

In the diary entries, a sense of her own real worth as a writer begins to appear, as well as her awareness of the difference between her writing and that of the mainstream. In the letters, she still teases her friends with exaggerated hopes and fears for her work, begging often to be contradicted, and fixating on one person's opinion; but in the diaries a more sober assessment emerges: "I look upon disregard or abuse as part of my bargain. I'm to write what I like; and they're to say what they like. My only interest as a writer lies, I begin to see, in some queer individuality; not in strength, or passion, or anything startling; but then I say to myself, is not 'some queer individuality' precisely the quality I respect?"

The strength of these statements comes from an inner certainty rather than a dependence on outer reassurance. This is when a writer's apprenticeship really comes to an end: when she can say to her public, or even privately, "I'm to write what I like; and they're to say what they like." It's like watching the moon sail free from behind a cloud.

The Hogarth Press became Leonard's main occupation from 1915 on. He had impulsively left the British civil service in Ceylon in 1911 to marry Virginia and was therefore out of a job. After World War I he began to move into politics, became the literary editor of the *Nation*, was involved in the League of Nations, and once was a Labour Party candidate to Parliament—all the while working constantly at the press. Virginia too worked constantly at the press, after mornings of writing. Her "room of one's own" became a small cubbyhole in a corner of Hogarth House, then later at Monk's House, Rodmell in Sussex, where she wrote and smoked and was available for questions from Leonard or one of their young assistants. She no longer—or not so often—raged about all the activity going on around her. Life was, after all, about books.

The first Hogarth Press publication, in 1917, was *Two Stories* by Virginia Woolf and L. S. Woolf: her "The Mark on the Wall" and his "Three Jews," with woodcut illustrations by Dora Carrington, who was an art student at the time. It announced their marriage as a partnership and as an imprint. Virginia had to learn typesetting because Leonard's hands shook too much; the tremor had been with him all his life. She spent days folding, stapling, and gluing books, and she took parcels to the post office herself. It was all immensely time-consuming, hard and grubby work. The "Woolves" were renowned for arriving late at dinner parties, their hands covered in ink, Virginia's hair a mess, and Leonard shaking like a leaf.

They published T. S. Eliot's poems and *The Waste Land*,

Katherine Mansfield's *Prelude*, and books by Middleton Murry, Edward Garnett, and Vita Sackville-West as well as Virginia's own work. They turned down James Joyce's *Ulysses*, mainly because of its length; later, she accused herself of not having appreciated Joyce. Much of the Hogarth Press's cover art was designed and drawn by Vanessa Bell, often in a postimpressionist style. Virginia wrote to Vanessa in 1918 about her illustration for "Kew Gardens": "I think the book will be a great success—owing to you; and my vision comes out much as I had it, so I suppose, in spite of everything, God made our brains upon the same lines, only leaving out 2 or 3 pieces in mine."

The cover drawings, which are in use to this day, show how in tune Vanessa was with her sister's vision of things. They are often domestic yet suggestive of an outside world beyond the object: a window, a door, a curtain, a bowl; an open line that both describes and includes. When Vanessa sent the cover art for *Jacob's Room*, Virginia wrote to her, "We think your design lovely. Our only doubts are practical. L. thinks the lettering isn't plain enough, and the effect is rather too dazzling. Could you make the r of Room into a Capital? These considerations may spoil the design though." Vanessa mostly complied, but the r in *A Room of One's Own* remained lowercase, as it is in *The Common Reader*, as Vanessa obviously preferred, using the style of the Omega Workshops.

The Hogarth Press began early to gain the reputation for modernism that has stayed with it now for a century. The writer John Lehmann, who was the managing editor from 1938 to 1946, claimed that many of its publishing decisions were revolutionary. It was part of the wave of independent-minded publications that flourished between 1910 and 1930: the *Dial*, the *Egoist*, the *Little Review*, Sylvia Beach's *Shakespeare and Company*. For Virginia Stephen, now Virginia Woolf, it provided the structure and base of her mature writing career and brought her the readers she deserved. Its familial nature—the Woolfs published many of their friends' work as well as unsolicited manuscripts—brought the press some criticism from outside but was also a source of its strength and unity of vision.

On January 26, 1920, Woolf wrote a diary entry that deserves to be quoted at length, since it shows so much of what she was thinking about form in the novel and about her own method (its "queer individuality"), which she was now able to explore and express:

> The day after my birthday: I'm 38, well, I've no doubt I'm a great deal happier than I was at 28, having this afternoon arrived at some idea of a new form for a new novel. Suppose one thing should open out of another—as in an unwritten novel—only not for 10 pages but 200 or so—doesn't that give the looseness and lightness I want; doesn't that get closer and yet keep form and speed, and enclose everything, everything? My doubt is how far it will enclose the human heart—Am I sufficiently mistress of my dialogue to net it there? For I figure that the approach will be entirely different this time; no scaffolding; scarcely a brick to be seen; all crepuscular, but the heart, the passion, humour, everything as bright as a fire in the mist. Then I'll find room for so much—a gaiety, an inconsequence—a light-spirited stepping at my sweet will. Whether I'm sufficiently mistress of things, that's the doubt; but conceive, Mark on the Wall, K.G. ["Kew Gardens"] and Unwritten Novel taking hands and dancing in unity. What the unity shall be I have yet to discover; the theme is a blank to me; but I see immense possibilities in the form I hit upon more or less by chance, two weeks ago. I suppose the danger is the damned egotistical self; which ruins [James] Joyce and [Dorothy] Richardson to my mind; is one pliant and rich enough to provide a wall for the book from oneself without its becoming, as in Joyce and Richardson, narrowing and restricting? My hope is that I've learnt my business sufficiently now to provide all sorts of entertainments. Anyhow I must still grope

and experiment, but this afternoon I had a gleam of light. Indeed, I think from the ease with which I'm developing the unwritten novel there must be a path for me there.

That April she began to write *Jacob's Room*. In early May
she wrote in her diary, "Directly one gets to work one is like
a person walking who has seen the countryside stretching out
before. I want to write nothing in this book that I don't enjoy
writing. Yet writing is always difficult."

I think these two diary extracts, written for herself, as one
writes diaries, but also with one eye on posterity, describe as
well as anything Virginia Woolf's arrival at the end of her long
apprenticeship. They were also (not coincidentally, I think)
written when she was deeply involved in part ownership of an
increasingly influential publishing house. She was making and
selling books as well as writing them. She had indeed "learnt
[her] business" in more ways than one.

Epilogue

All this exploration of Virginia's early life, influences, states of mind, places, and history feels, in the end, like only a warm-up. How did she do it? How did Virginia Stephen become that great mind, that great writer, that innovative modernist, the visionary Virginia Woolf? It wasn't by marrying Leonard Woolf, or by becoming one of "the Woolves," as they called themselves. It wasn't by owning a publishing house, by knowing great men and women, or by writing hundreds of letters to them. It wasn't by traveling, staying home, entertaining, or having an early night. It wasn't by reading all the great writers who came before her, reviewing them, or looking at postimpressionist paintings in exhibitions. It wasn't by running around London or staying home. It wasn't because of her parents, her ancestors, her beloved sister, her lost brother, or her ghosts. It was the result of something that escapes the bounds of ordinary life and evades all explanation. It is what happens inside the head and body of a writer when she writes. It's irreducible, really. It doesn't depend on circumstance, opportunity, hard work, or respect for a routine, even though all these may help. It can't be produced by the will, a decision, or even by showing up at the page.

Considering all the aspects of Virginia Stephen's young life —seeing what she struggled with, what amused her and made her happy, and what cast her down—I still come up against the awed realization that this was the childhood and youth of an extraordinary being and that what is at the center of great writing, what we call genius, is still inexplicable. There is something given, something unknowable, that comes from far outside oneself and from deep inside at the same time. Nobody has ever defined it. So many people have written about Virginia Woolf, trying to pin her down—investigating her tastes, her limitations, her illnesses, her loves, her sexuality, and so on—but it can't be done, I think. We can know so much about her life; she left a mass of evidence, in all the volumes of the letters that have survived, the diaries, the notes, the essays, the reviews, the short stories, and finally, the novels themselves. But she didn't leave us a key to it all—not in the sense that we can use it to turn in a keyhole and open the door upon her genius. I think she didn't understand it herself. Perhaps no artist ever does.

Where does it come from, the desire that becomes an urge that becomes words, flying one after another, or becomes paint on a canvas, creating something that simply wasn't in the world before? We can analyze, subtract, and divide; we can take things apart and examine the brushstrokes, the words on the page, or the marks on the music sheet; but we can't ever really know. Woolf herself used analogy and image to come as close as she could to the process, the surrender to the process, and then the consummation of the mark on the page. She knew of what she spoke, but she couldn't analyze or reduce it. It exists in her work: Lily Briscoe by the shore, looking out to the lighthouse, seeing the boat arrive, being visited by the ghost of Mrs. Ramsay; the vision of Bernard, the writer, in *The Waves*; Mrs. Dalloway, stepping out into the newness of a London morning to buy the flowers herself; Jacob waking to another day in his childhood room.

We go back to these moments and know that they have immeasurably lit and enriched our own lives. As writers, we long to produce the same effect. But all we can know, really, is the intense desire and the long process that may or may not end in "getting there." All we can do is sit in the chair, at the desk, and try—"stone-breaking," even (see chapter 8)—and then, when the time is right, stop trying and trust, as Virginia Woolf did, that we can perhaps take flight.

She gave clues to younger writers, during her lifetime. Her own letters to young poets—mostly written to Julian Bell and Gerald Brenan—express many of her own "young" thoughts and dilemmas. What she passed on to the recipients remains pertinent to later generations.

She wrote to her nephew Julian in 1926, commenting on his poems, "I think you will have to learn to leave out details, even though they are good in themselves." In a letter to Gerald in 1929 she confided, "You say you can't finish your book because you have no method but see points here and there with no connecting line. And that is precisely my state. The will o' the wisp moves on and I see the lights, as bright as stars, and cant reach them. I thought anyhow I had learnt to write quickly; now it's a hundred words in a morning, and scratchy and in [hand]writing like a child of ten. And one never knows after all these years how to end, how to go on: one never sees more than a page ahead."

This is how Virginia Woolf connected with me as a beginning writer, and still does: you never know quite where you are going, but you never give up, and you go there anyway. Then, if you persist, something happens, and you may find you are indeed flying, not "stone-breaking." You are in a process, with few guidelines except your own desire and your own patchy belief in what you are doing; but you have her witty, self-deprecating voice at your ear, reminding you that this is how it is. Like life, writing has no easy answers, no guidelines, and no way of ever seeing more than a page ahead. This is what Woolf can give to young writers today—as she did to the worried Gerald Brenan writing to her from his mountaintop in

Spain and as she did to me as a young writer, fifty years ago, on my bus traveling to work. You can feel like a complete failure, as she often did, but you do it anyway.

I would like to end with Virginia Woolf's diary entry of Saturday, February 7, 1931, recording the finishing of *The Waves*:

> Here in the few minutes that remain, I must record, heaven be praised, the end of "The Waves." I wrote the last words O Death fifteen minutes ago, having reeled across the last ten pages with some moments of such intensity and intoxication that I seemed only to stumble after my own voice, or almost, after some sort of speaker (as when I was mad) I was almost afraid, remembering the voices that used to fly ahead. Anyhow it is done; and I have been sitting these 15 minutes in a state of glory, and calm, and some tears, thinking of Thoby and if I could write Julian Thoby Stephen 1881–1906 on the first page. I suppose not. How physical the sense of triumph and relief is! Whether good or bad, it's done; and as I certainly felt at the end, not merely finished, but rounded off, completed, the thing stated—how hastily, how fragmentarily I know; but I mean that I have netted that fin in the waste of water which appeared to me over the marshes out of my window at Rodmell when I was coming to an end of To the Lighthouse.

Can one come any closer to her than this?

Notes

Most of the quotations in this volume are taken from Virginia's early correspondence and from her diaries. After providing a full citation for each volume, I have used the following abbreviations:

DVW = Virginia Woolf. *The Diary of Virginia Woolf.* 5 vols. Edited by Anne Olivier Bell. New York: Harvest Books, 1979–1985. (Citations include diary entry date.)

LVW = Virginia Woolf. *The Letters of Virginia Woolf.* 6 vols. Edited by Nigel Nicholson and Joanne Trautmann. New York: Harvest Books, 1975–1982. (Citations include letter number.)

WD = Virginia Woolf. *A Writer's Diary: Being Extracts from the Diary of Virginia Woolf.* Edited by Leonard Woolf. New York: Harvest Books, 1954. (Citations include page number.)

INTRODUCTION

1, "The sun had not yet risen": Virginia Woolf, *The Waves* (London: Hogarth Press, 1931), 1.

2, "As it happened": Eudora Welty, "Foreword," in Virginia Woolf, *To the Lighthouse* (New York: Harcourt Brace Jovanovich, 1989), vii.

4, "I always read Montaigne": Virginia Woolf, *Letters of Virginia Woolf,* vol. 1, *1888–1912,* ed. Nigel Nicholson and Joanne Trautmann (New York: Harvest Books, 1975), letter 66. (Hereafter LVW 1:letter no.)

4, "my real delight": LVW 1:202, to Madge Vaughan, 1904.

4, "reading Henry James": Ibid.

5, "I'm going to write": LVW 1:57.

5, "Oh how I wish": LVW 1:477.

CHAPTER 1 · Expectations

9, "I want to see how quick": LVW 1:2.

9, "The beauty of my language": LVW 1:5.

10, "My dear Dr. Seton": LVW 1:6.

10, "Think how I was brought up": Virginia Woolf, *The Letters of Virginia Woolf*, vol. 3, 1923–1928, ed. Nigel Nicholson and Joanne Trautmann (New York: Harvest Books, 1980), 1624. (Hereafter LVW 3:letter no.)

10, "regular as a Clock": LVW 1:107, to Violet Dickinson, 1903.

10, "Your talk is as good": LVW 1:156.

10, "I had a letter": LVW 1:444.

11, "Janet C. said ": LVW 1:576.

11, "He wanted something": Woolf, *Lighthouse*, 123.

11, "Thoby is here today": LVW 1:28.

11, "Father is stretched": LVW 1:29.

12, "Nessa is like a great child": LVW 1:381.

12, "Father has begun to say": LVW 1:36.

14, "He has written a novel": LVW 1:629, to Lady Robert Cecil, 1912.

14, "I dont think I will come": LVW 1:43.

14, "My mind is dazed": LVW 1:47.

15, "All these years": LVW 1:165.

CHAPTER 2 · Reading

17, "my beloved Macaulay": LVW 1:6, to Thoby Stephen, 1897.

18, "Imogen says": LVW 1:39.

18, "I think he is about the greatest": LVW 1:333.

18, "I have been reading": LVW 1:355.

18, " cheerful manly books": LVW 1:380, to Violet Dickinson, 1907.

19, "I am climbing Moore": LVW 1:426.

20, "I dont [sic] get anyone to argue": LVW 1:81.

21, "You are an angel": LVW 1:66.

21, "Even in virtue": Michel de Montaigne, *The Essays: A Selection*, ed. M. A. Screech (New York: Penguin Books, 1993), 18.

21, "I want death": Ibid., 62.

22, "trivial ephemeral books": Virginia Woolf, "The Lives of the Obscure," in *The Essays of Virginia Woolf*, vol. 4, *1925–1928*, ed. Andrew McNeillie (London: Hogarth Press, 1994), 140.

22, "I ransack public libraries": Ibid.

22, "All her generation": Virginia Woolf, *The Diary of Virginia Woolf*, vol. 1, *1915–1919*, ed. Anne Olivier Bell (New York: Harvest Books, 1979), September 10, 1918. (Hereafter *DVW* 1: entry date.)

22, Virginia was a lifelong supporter: Hermione Lee, *Virginia Woolf* (New York: Vintage Press, 1997), 414.

23, "Oh dear, what a lot": *DVW* 1: March 5, 1919.

23, "I like it less": E. M. Forster, quoted in Virginia Woolf, *A Writer's Diary: Being Extracts from the Diary of Virginia Woolf*, ed. Leonard Woolf (New York: Harvest Books, 1954), 19. (Hereafter *WD* with page number.)

23, "suddenly out comes": *WD*, ibid.

CHAPTER 3 · Writing

25, "My dear godpapa": LVW 1:1.

25, "A thousand thanks": LVW 1:4.

26, "Sparroy says it's a question": LVW 1:355.

26, "Thoby is going on well": LVW 1:318.

26, "He begins to curse": LVW 1:319.

27, "Do you hate me": LVW 1:326.

27, "When I read the thing": LVW 1:471.

28, "There should be threads": LVW 1:480.

28, "Writing is a divine art": LVW 1:250.

28, "Do you think": Ibid.

29, "It seems to me": LVW 1:272.

29, "When I see a pen and ink": LVW 1:203.

29, "The first really *lived* year": DVW 1: January 1, 1897; quoted in preface, vii.

30, "Never mind": DVW 1: July 20, 1897; quoted in preface, vii.

30, "The diary is too personal": WD, ix.

31, "keep myself in pocket money": LVW 1:206.

31, "I don't want": LVW 1:191.

32, "I stupidly didn't typewrite": Ibid.

32, "I must toil": LVW 1:192.

32, "Without a word": LVW 1:206.

32, "a little cause for joy": LVW 1:217.

33, "I am realizing": LVW 1: 218.

33, "Of this novel": Virginia Woolf, "A Dark Lantern," in *The Essays of Virginia Woolf*, vol. 1, *1904-1912*, ed. Andrew McNeillie (New York: Harcourt, 1987), 42.

34, "Miss McCracken": Virginia Woolf, "The American Woman," in ibid., 46.)

34, "Almost all essays": Virginia Woolf, "The Decay of Essay-Writing," in ibid., 25.

35, "I learnt a lot": Virginia Woolf, *The Diary of Virginia Woolf*, vol. 5, *1936-1941*, ed. Anne Olivier Bell (New York: Harvest Books, 1985), May 5, 1938.

35, "I really believe": LVW 1:408, to Lytton Strachey, 1908.

35, "I always think": LVW 1:88.

35, "We went and had tea": LVW 1:380.

36, "The problem before the novelist": Virginia Woolf, "Modern Novels," *Times Literary Supplement*, April 10, 1919.

CHAPTER 4 · Looking and Listening

37, "Looking, looking, looking": LVW 3:1730.

37, "My meticulous observations": DVW 1: August 7, 1918.

37, "They play the piano": LVW 1:222.

37, "serious noticing": James Wood, *The Nearest Thing to Life* (Waltham, MA: Brandeis University Press, 2015), 58.

37, "infinite strange shapes": LVW 1:438, to Clive Bell, 1908.

38, "At this very moment": Virginia Woolf, *The Letters of Virginia Woolf*, vol. 2, *1912–1922*, ed. Nigel Nicholson and Joanne Trautmann (New York: Harvest Books, 1976), 645. (Hereafter LVW 2:letter no.)

38, "Think of orange trees": LVW 1:224.

39, "fin in the waste": WD, 165.

40, "I think a great deal": LVW 1:438.

40, "semi-transparent envelope": Woolf, "Modern Novels."

41, "Is it not possible": Ibid.

41, "Ah, it is the sea": LVW 1:438.

CHAPTER 5 · The Place

47, "as if issued": Virginia Woolf, *Mrs. Dalloway* (New York: Penguin, 1992), 1.

47, "If life has a base": Virginia Woolf, "A Sketch of the Past," in *Moments of Being: Unpublished Autobiographical Writings*, ed. Jeanne Schulkind (New York: Harcourt Brace Jovanovich, 1976), 73.

49, "Ka wants me to lunch": LVW 2:1171.

CHAPTER 6 · Family and Friends

51, "I am feeling really quiet": LVW 1:189.

51, "We have begun": LVW 1:188.

52, "humdrum little society": LVW 1:188.

52, "makes me consider": DVW 1: October 23, 1918.

53, "At your age": Quoted in Lee, *Virginia Woolf*, 209.

53, "No one really takes": LVW 1:250.

53, "We were full": Virginia Woolf, "Old Bloomsbury," in *Moments of Being*, ed. Schulkind, 185.

55, "I shall want": LVW 1:333.

55, "The world is full": LVW 1:334.

55, "It is very hard": LVW 1:346.

55, "Nessa still writes": LVW 1:347.

56, "We had very successful travels": LVW 1:449.

56, "We had Lytton": LVW 1:462.

57, "It's odd, retiring": LVW 1:563.

58, "I was glad": DVW 1: November 1 or 2, 1917.

CHAPTER 7 · Routine

59, "The astonishing thing": LVW 1:371.

60, "Our London season": LVW 1:37.

61, "Generalisations bring back": Virginia Woolf, "The Mark on the Wall," in *The Collected Short Stories of Virginia Woolf* (n.p.: Oxford City Press, 2011), 9.

62, "We both of us want": LVW 1:615.

62, "We're both writing": LVW 1:633.

62, "I write all the morning": LVW 1:563.

62, "Happiness—what, I wonder": DVW 1: May 7, 1919.

63, "All the eating and drinking": LVW 1:531.

CHAPTER 8 · "That Dangerous Ground"

65, "that dangerous ground": Virginia Woolf, *The Letters of Virginia Woolf*, vol. 4, *1929-1931*, ed. Nigel Nicholson and Joanne Trautmann (New York: Harvest Books, 1981), 2254, to Ethel Smyth, 1930. (Hereafter LVW 4:letter no.)

66, "The death intensified": Lee, *Virginia Woolf*, 223.

67, "After being ill": LVW 4:2254.

68, "Turning her eyes": Virginia Woolf, *The Voyage Out* (New York: Oxford University Press, 1997), 382.

68, "little deformed women": Ibid., 386.

68, "Thought had ceased": Ibid.

CHAPTER 9 · The First Novel

71, "It was this sea that": Woolf, *Voyage Out*, 210.

71, "I shall be miserable": LVW 1:369.

71, "A narrative should be as straight": LVW 1:371.

72, "I feel like one rolled": LVW 1:377.

72, "My writing makes me tremble": LVW 1:389.

72, "I dreamt last night": LVW 1:406.

73, "It comes over me": Ibid.

73, "O I have been so peevish": LVW 1:428.

73, "Ah well!": LVW 1:442.

73, "Yesterday I finished": LVW 1:566.

74, "Every morning I write": LVW 1:618.

74, "he is far and away": LVW 1:621.

74, "By the way": LVW 1:625.

74, "He has written": LVW 1:629.

75, "I'm the only woman": Virginia Woolf, *The Diary of Virginia Woolf*, vol. 3, *1925–1930*, ed. Anne Olivier Bell (New York: Harvest Books, 1981), September 22, 1925.

75, "I'll send you my book": LVW 2:1272.

76, "Why, if one wants to compare": Woolf "Mark on the Wall," 6–7; ellipsis in the original.

77, "Style is a very simple matter": LVW 3:1624.

79, "There's no doubt": WD, 46.

79, "My proofs come": Ibid., 48.

80, "A mildly unfavorable review": Ibid., 43.

80, "Women can't write": Woolf, *Lighthouse*, 48.

80, "I look upon disregard": WD, 43–44.

82, "I think the book": LVW 2:985.

82, "We think your design": Ibid.

83, "The day after": WD, 25.

84, "Directly one gets to work": Ibid.

EPILOGUE

87, "I think you will have to learn": LVW 3:1823.

87, "You say you can't finish": LVW 4:2078.

88, "Here in the few minutes": WD, 165.

Index

the Nation, 81
National Review, 31, 32–33
Nevill, Dorothy, 35
new and old, tension between,
    40–41
newspapers, writing for, 32
Night and Day, 23, 67, 75–76, 78
novel writing, 40–41, 57. See also
    fiction

objectivity, 24
observations, 37–42
Omega Workshops, 39, 40, 82
organized labor, 11
Orlando, 31
ornithology, 19
Oxford University, 12–13

painterly description, 41–42
painters and painting, 39–40, 54
Paris, 56
Pasolini, Pier Paolo, 48
Pater, Clara, 18
Pepys, Samuel, 17
place, 43–49
poetry, 71
Porthminster, 47
Porthminster Hotel, 49
Portugal, 37, 38
postimpressionism, 39–40
post-traumatic stress disorder
    (PTSD), 69
potentiality, 66
Pound, Ezra, 23
prose style, 71, 76–77
Proust, Marcel, 48, 49

"queer individuality," 80, 83

Raverat, Jacques, 39, 40, 54
reading, 3–4, 9, 12–13, 17–24, 57;
    experience and, 22; loneliness
    of, 20; as routine, 62; thorough,
    19–20; as a writer, 17
realism, 67, 71
regimen, 59–63
reviews, 23–24, 28
rhythm, 76–77
Richardson, Dorothy, 65, 83
Richmond, Bruce, 32–33, 34–35
Richmond, home in, 75
Robins, Elizabeth, 33
Rodmell, house at, 21
A Room of One's Own, 20, 82
Roosevelt, Theodore, 35
routine, 59–63
Rye, 19

Sackville-West, Vita, 10, 37, 77, 82
Sand, George, 20
scene setting, 41
the sea, 41–42, 71
seaside memories, 43–44
self-doubt, 80
"serious noticing," 37
Seton, Dr., 10
Shakespeare, William, 18, 21
Sickert, Walter, 54
"A Sketch of the Past," 47–48
Slade School of Fine Art, 15
Smith, Reginald, 35
Smyth, Ethel, 67
solitude, need for, 58
Sophocles, 12
Spain, 37, 38–39
St. Erth, 43
St. Ives, 43–48, 49, 65, 72
Steiner, George, 2
Stephen (Bell), Vanessa, 3, 7, 14,

15–16, 17, 25, 27, 39–40, 61, 66; abstract painting style of, 39; artwork for Hogarth Press, 82; at Bloomsbury, 52, 53–54; as example to Virginia, 12; Friday club for artists at Bloomsbury, 52, 53–54; illness in Constantinople, 52; illustration for "Kew Gardens," 82; marriage of, 12, 13, 54–56; paintings of, 54; routine and, 59, 61; studies painting, 15; Virginia's correspondence with, 10–11, 49, 56–57, 63, 73, 82; youth of, 17, 18

Stephen (Woolf), Virginia, 2, 7, 66; activism of, 11; advice for young writers, 87–88; anticipates her own death, 66; apprenticeship to the novel, 75–76, 79, 81, 84; becoming Virginia Woolf, 85; capacity for work, 35; childlessness of, 12, 62; death of, 48; diet of, 60, 63; education of, 3–4, 5, 7, 10, 12–13, 18–20; expectations of, 9–16, 71; expectations of herself, 15; health of, 7; at Hogarth Press, 81–84; instability of, 62; at King's College, 10; learns typesetting, 81; Leonard proposes to, 74; marriage of, 10, 13–14, 20–21, 58, 61–62, 67, 74–75, 81; marriage proposals received by, 10, 53; meets and marries Leonard Woolf, 10, 13–14, 20–21, 74–75; mental illness and, 60, 63, 66–69; mentors of, 15; molested by half brothers, 6; moves to Fitzroy Square, 54, 56; moves to Little Talland House, 56–57; need for independence, 62; refers to diary as "sketchbook,"

54; routine and, 59–63; self-criticism, 15; sends first novel to Duckworth Press, 13; suffers pangs of beginning writers, 32–33; teaching at Morley College, 54; transformation into Virginia Woolf, 3–4; youth of, 6, 9–18, 19, 23, 25, 43–48, 49, 59–63, 65, 85–86. *See also* Woolf, Virginia, works of

Stephen, Adrian, 7, 19, 37, 38–39, 54, 55, 56, 66, 74

Stephen, Julia, 43; death of, 6–7, 10, 11, 49, 59, 65, 66–67; reading to her children, 17

Stephen, Leslie, 4, 6, 11, 43, 49, 73; bereavement of, 11; death of, 6, 7, 15, 51, 61, 65, 67; as editor of *National Dictionary of Biography*, 9, 15; emotional dependence and demands of, 11, 21; expectations of, 12–13, 71; influence of, 15, 35; legacy of, 14; letters of, 32; library of, 9, 17

Stephen, Thoby, 4, 6, 7, 11, 12, 27, 66; at Bloomsbury, 53–54; death of, 6, 7, 27, 52, 53, 54–55, 65, 66, 88; education of, 12, 18; expectations of, 12; illness in Constantinople, 52; influence of, 18; Virginia's correspondence with, 9–10, 14–15, 20, 21, 25, 26, 51; Virginia's intellectual companionship with, 27

Stephen family, 13, 17, 32, 44, 66; at Bloomsbury, 51–53; at St. Ives, 43–48, 49, 72. *See also specific family members*

Stevenson, Robert Louis, 18–19

Strachey, Lytton, 20, 28, 51, 53, 56, 72

Strachey, Marjorie, 54
Swinburne, Algernon Charles, 28

talk, 62
Talland House, Cornwall, England, 43, 44–45, 46, 48, 49, 68
Thackeray, William, 17
"that dangerous ground," 65–69
Thoreau, Henry David, 18–19
Three Guineas, 20
time, balancing, 57–58
Times Literary Supplement, 31, 32–33, 34, 36
To the Lighthouse, 2, 7, 11, 17, 39, 45–47, 49, 80, 86, 88; death in, 65–66; legacy of Leslie Stephen in, 14–15; painters and painting in, 54; prose style of 76–77
Tonks, Henry, 15
tragedy, 7
traveling, 37, 38–39, 52, 56
Trinity College, 25
Trollope, Anthony, 18
Twickenham, nursing home in, 63
Two Stories (with L. S. Woolf), 81
typesetting, 81

University of East Anglia, 16
"An Unwritten Novel," 39, 67, 83
ur-memory, 48

Vaughan, Emma, 11, 25, 33, 60
Vaughan, Madge, 5, 28–29, 31, 51–52, 55
vision, 76, 78
the visual, 40–41
The Voyage Out, 7, 23, 37, 62, 68, 71–78

walking, 62
water, 48
Watts, George Frederick, 54
The Waves, 1, 2–3, 39, 46–48, 65–66, 77, 86, 88
Wells, H. G., 41
Wells, Somerset, 73
Welty, Eudora, 2
Whistler, James McNeill, exhibition at New Gallery, 54
womanhood, Victorian ideal of, 11
women: careers of, 15; obligations of, 59–60; permitted genres, 14; as writers, 14, 79–84
women's suffrage, 11
Wood, James, 37
Woolf, Leonard, 13, 14, 20–21, 38, 57, 58, 60, 63, 80, 85; in civil service in Ceylon, 53; dependability of, 61; edition of Virginia's diaries, 29, 30; at Hogarth Press, 81, 82–83; involved in League of Nations, 81; as literary editor for the *Nation*, 81; marriage of, 67; politics and, 81; proposes to Virginia, 74; returns from Ceylon, 74; "Three Jews," 81; Virginia's correspondence with, 61–62
Woolf, Virginia. *See* Stephen (Woolf), Virginia; Woolf, Virginia, works of
Woolf, Virginia, works of: anonymous contribution to Frederic Maitland's *Life and Letters of Sir Leslie Stephen*, 9; *The Common Reader*, 82; "The Decay of Essay Writing," 34; diaries of, 22, 25, 29–31, 37, 52–53, 54, 58, 77, 79, 80–81, 83–84, 88;

early writings, 5; essays by, 31–36; "Hayworth," 31; *Jacob's Room*, 7, 37–38, 46, 65–66, 68–69, 75, 79, 82, 84, 86; "Kew Gardens," 39, 82, 83; letters of, 5, 9–11, 14–15, 18–21, 25–29, 37–39, 41–42, 49, 51, 55–56, 60–62, 71–74, 77, 80, 82, 87–88; *To the Lighthouse*, 2, 7, 11, 14–15, 17, 39, 45–47, 49, 54, 65–66, 76–77, 80, 86, 88; "The Mark on the Wall," 39, 61, 76, 81, 83; "Melymbrosia" (*The Voyage Out*), 27, 62, 72–73; memoir about her father, 9; "Memoirs of a Novelist," 35; memoirs of Sarah Bernhardt and Dorothy Nevill, 35; mentors of, 22, 34–35 (*see also* specific mentors); "Modern Novels," 36, 41; *Mrs. Dalloway*, 7, 47, 65–66, 69, 77, 79, 86; *Night and Day*, 23, 67, 75–76, 78; *Orlando*, 31; "Phyllis and Rosamond," 51–52; published by Hogarth Press, 81–82; reviews by, 25, 31–36, 80; reviews of, 23, 31; *A Room of One's Own*, 20, 82; self-criticism, 28; "A Sketch of the Past," 47–48; *Three Guineas*, 20; *Two Stories* (with L. S. Woolf), 81; "An Unwritten Novel," 39, 67, 83; *The Voyage Out*, 7, 23, 37, 62, 68, 71–78; *The Waves*, 1, 2–3, 39, 46, 47, 48, 65–66, 77, 86, 88

World War I, 80, 81

World War II, 80

writers, reading, 17; women as, 14, 79–84

writing, 25–36; about what you do or do not know, 72; balancing time of, 57–58; becoming a writer, 3–9, 11, 13–14, 16, 19–20, 85; description, 37–42; desire to write, 86–87; marriage and, 74–75; mental illness and, 67–69; routine and, 59–63; spurred by loss, 49; technique, 76–77

"writing school," 16

Zennor, Cornwall, 49

MUSE BOOKS
The Iowa Series in Creativity and Writing
. . . .